Cooperative Learning Throughout the Year

Helping Young Children Work Together

by Jeri A. Carroll
and
Marcia Seaton

illustrated by Becky J. Radtke

Cover by Becky J. Radtke

Copyright © Good Apple, 1992

ISBN No. 0-86653-663-9

Printing No. 987654321

Good Apple
1204 Buchanan St., Box 299
Carthage, IL 62321-0299

SIMON & SCHUSTER *A Paramount Communications Company*

Dedication

Cooperative learning actively involves children working together in small groups to attain a common goal while practicing language, problem solving, thinking and decision-making skills. Strategies, experienced and learned at an early age, can then be utilized whenever needed. Children's creativity and a positive self-concept develop as a result of information gathering through cooperation.

This book is dedicated to our families, teachers, colleagues and students who supported our cooperative venture in designing these activities for young children. We further dedicate this book to those teachers who implement and evaluate these activities allowing young children to reap the benefits, learning to get along.

GA1395

Table of Contents

GA1395

GA1395

Introduction

JUST WHAT IS COOPERATIVE LEARNING?

Cooperative learning is a teaching strategy that involves children of all performance levels working together in small groups to reach a common goal. The process used in reaching the goal may be the most valuable element to the child's development of social skills and academic skills.

Cooperative learning is relatively inexpensive to implement into the existing curriculum. It can increase motivation to learn by adding variety to teaching methods and allows for different learning styles and performance levels of each individual's unique needs. Once cooperative learning strategies are learned, teachers can also introduce new content using these strategies.

Cooperative learning creates opportunities for the exchange of more and better ideas rather than working alone or competitively. All subject areas and grade levels can be taught using this strategy. Cooperative learning requires careful planning, organization and constant monitoring for successful results.

GA1395

WHY COOPERATIVE LEARNING WITH YOUNG CHILDREN?

Young children learn best when allowed to interact positively with others in their environment. Cooperative learning provides experiences that develop language skills, thinking and problem solving skills, social skills and academic skills. Research suggests that children working together in small groups develop higher self-esteem, a greater concern for others and higher academic achievement. Although most cooperative learning research has been done with children of second grade to adults in college, it applies to young children as well.

The Developmentally Appropriate Practice in Early Childhood Programs Serving Children from Birth Through Age 8 (published by NAEYC) suggests that teachers should prepare the environment for children to learn through active exploration and interaction with adults, other children and materials. Teachers are also encouraged to facilitate the development of cooperating, helping, negotiating and talking with others. Many states are encouraging, through mandates, the use of cooperative learning in math, writing and reading.

In today's world many children come to school already identified as "at-risk students," and yet still many children are full of curiosity and filled with a desire to learn. Educators feel a greater need than ever before to increase time on task, establish better discipline and improve motivation to learn. Cooperative learning activities should be planned to provide direct experiences that allow positive interaction of children and learning as well.

Attitudes and skills are constantly being developed during a child's first few years of life and provide the formation of a framework for further thinking and how to function within the world. How better to form them than in the early childhood classroom as children who may live together as adults learn to work and play together.

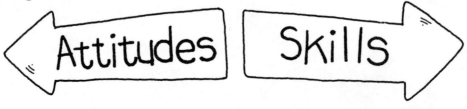

GA1395

WAYS TO PRESENT COOPERATIVE LEARNING TO YOUNG CHILDREN

GROUPING OF CHILDREN

Group Size

The size of the cooperative learning group is determined by the teacher after selecting the lesson content, determining the objective for the lesson, setting the criteria for mastery of the objective and designing the activity that will be used to develop the desired learning. Group size will vary according to the number of tasks, requirements of tasks and the amount of time available for the activity.

Group Makeup

The teacher decides which children will be in a group by selecting children of various performance levels, different sexes and different ethnic backgrounds. Behavior of children may also be considered when selecting children for a group. Cooperative learning activities can make children feel a part of the class and reduce discipline problems in the classroom.

Use heterogeneous grouping when selecting small groups of children. When considering performance, select high-, medium-, and low-performance levels for a group of three children. A group of four children would have one high-, one low- and two medium-performance level children when possible.

Paired Instruction

When dividing groups of children into pairs, it is best to select students with high- and medium-performance levels or low- and medium-performance levels. Often a pair of extreme high- and extreme low-performance level children seem to have more conflicts and less positive interaction. Consider using pairs of children when organizing cooperative learning experiences for the first few times.

GA1395

Working in Small Groups

Many activities lend themselves to young children working together in groups of three or four children. Each child must have a specific task. Clear instructions from the teacher are necessary to assure that each child understands his/her task.

Some of the activities in this book have badges that children wear to show what their responsibilities are. When there are only two people in the group, children must remember their responsibilities (with a little help from their partners, of course).

JIGSAW WITH YOUNG CHILDREN

Jigsaw was originally used as a cooperative learning strategy at the secondary and college level. Each cooperative learning group had an expert who learned the information from a group of experts and took the information back to the learning group. The simple addition of giving young children badges and giving them a group and task assignment, makes this type of grouping work with young children who are still using only beginning reading skills.

When using Jigsaw with young children, children are assigned to a group of three or four. The group is color-coded and designated to be the home or family group. Assignment to groups is clear since each child will then wear a badge of a special color. Each member of the family group is also given a special task. The colored badge also has a symbol or picture of the child's special task.

A new group called the "expert group" is formed comprised of all the children who wear the same "expert" task symbol. This group learns new material or tasks. When their instruction is complete, members of the "expert group" return to the original groups. They share materials or information with their family groups to help them complete the new task. Completed activities can be shared with the whole class of children by discussing and displaying products.

4

GA1395

ASSEMBLY LINES

During assembly lines, children also have special tasks. The tasks can be labelled on the table, or the child may wear a badge. The tasks are named. The number of children in an assembly line is usually four to eight, depending on the activity and the number of products to be produced. Numbers may be assigned to keep the tasks in sequence.

Expectations for each group are important, but children begin to realize what cooperation is all about in assembly line activities. Each child will feel special if his task is special and vital to the success of the product. The process and product are both very important in this type of grouping.

Assembly line activities may require some expense, depending on the product.

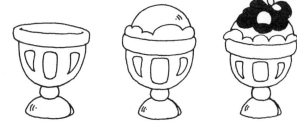

WORKING TOGETHER IN GROUPS

Each child should always know his/her task and have something valuable to do. Checking responses of others, cutting materials and sorting all may be tasks, and each is seen as critical. Young children may need different colored necklaces, headbands or badges to help children in the group know who has each task. Symbols may be required to designate a task. Monitoring is easily implemented when a visual is available to know immediately which task a child has been assigned.

TIME MANAGEMENT

When planning a cooperative learning lesson, determine the approximate time needed to complete the activity and allow a bit more for set up and for clean up. Schedule the activity during a time period that allows flexibility for additional time, if needed. Guide children to use time wisely, but do not rush through the activity. Don't be surprised if the children want to repeat the task several times. Be sure you allow repetition for feelings of competence.

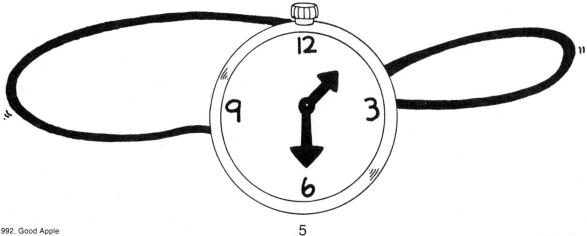

5

GA1395

WORKPLACES

Organization of the cooperative learning groups within the physical environment of the classroom depends on the specific activity. The teacher must be able to move within and around the cooperative learning groups to monitor constantly and provide guidance when needed. Sometimes groups may need to be in close proximity with other groups or as far away as possible.

It is all right for children to borrow an idea that is overheard or observed from a nearby group, since competition is not a factor. Young children in groups work well on the floor or at small tables. Centers within a classroom environment may be areas that children consider to be special work-places.

MONITORING COOPERATIVE LEARNING GROUPS AND ACTIVITIES

Monitoring should be constant during cooperative learning activities. The teacher monitors how the children are working together, as well as the product being constructed or task being completed. During the activity, the teacher acts as a guide and offers questions and assistance when needed, while still allowing children to solve problems successfully on their own as much as possible. When monitoring and observing, praise children for good behavior and good performance, encourage them to continue to work and be cooperative. Positive comments set the stage for more appropriate behavior to continue.

GA1395

BEHAVIOR MANAGEMENT

Expectations of behavior should be set and consistent within the classroom. Established classroom rules should be incorporated into cooperative learning activities. Examples of rules that work well with young children are: Use quiet voices, stay at your workplace, work together, help one another and say nice words to others.

PEER TEACHING

The value of peer teaching cannot be stressed enough. Time available to each child on a one-to-one basis with the teacher is never enough. In peer teaching there is a stated objective, and children work together to reach that objective. The building of lasting friendships and the enjoyment of working with someone else to solve problems enhances learning for many who are frustrated working alone or competitively.

SHARING TIME

It is critical to bring the children together at the end of a cooperative learning activity to bring closure to the cooperative learning lesson. Children are asked to share experiences and products with children from other groups. If these comments show displeasure, concern, aggravation, etc., with the task, teachers can solicit input from them on what changes might need to be made. If they show delight, teachers can file the task for use with next year's group, put it out for children to use again, or use the same strategy with another topic later in the year.

Teachers have time during this closure activity to give verbal praise for successful group work and, when appropriate, other rewards for good performance.

GA1395

ANALYSIS AND PLANNING

There is still one more step left after the cooperative lesson and group conference are finished. The lesson is analyzed in terms of how it went from the teacher's perspective. Did implementation of the lesson progress smoothly? Did the desired learning occur? How does the lesson need to be revised before it is taught again? And ask yourself—what will the next cooperative lesson be?

SUCCESS

Cooperative learning is a teaching strategy that promotes success. If one child's success leads to more children being successful, then our time is being wisely spent.

BOOK FORMAT

Cooperative Learning Throughout the Year is set up with four to five cooperative learning activities provided around themes that are typically studied during a particular month. For example, September's activities use the theme of friends, zoos and scarecrows. December's use wrapping presents, trimming trees and gingerbread cookies.

Each activity suggests something fun for children to do and shows teachers how some of the activities that they now do can be modified to include cooperative learning aspects. In addition, patterns for the badges or activity names are included. In some cases a follow-up activity serves as a reinforcement take-home paper which will stimulate conversation between the child and adult.

The take-home paper has one set of instructions at the top of the page. These can be used with younger children. If the children are younger, cover the directions at the bottom of the page before you copy it.

Older children have a second activity to do on the bottom of each take-home page. Typically it is an open-ended activity, while the first activity is a bit more controlled.

GA1395

Frog and Toad Together

Getting off to a good start when school begins is sometimes very difficult. Working in pairs will help children get acquainted, follow simple directions, give simple directions and find friends.

Materials Needed:

frog and toad headbands (see next page). One-half of the class will have green (frogs), and one-half of the class will have brown (toads).

Children can make these during an activity period the day before.

Preparing for the Lesson:

During circle time, read *Frog and Toad Together* by Arnold Lobel.

Grouping the Children:

Grouped in pairs, one member wears a frog headband and one wears a toad headband. Have the children sit facing one another.

Directed Activity:

The teacher reads the following instructions to the children.

Frog, say your name. Toad, say your name.

Frog, hop one time if Toad is wearing red.

Toad, hop two times if Frog is wearing green.

Toad, clap your hands two times if Frog is wearing a belt.

Frog, clap your hands one time if Toad is wearing tennis shoes.

Frog, stamp your foot if Toad is wearing any circles.

Toad, stamp your foot if Frog has brown hair.

Toad, turn around one time if Frog has red hair.

Frog, pat your head if Toad has any sisters.

Toad, pat your shoulder if Frog has any brothers.

Frog, say Toad's name.

Toad, say Frog's name.

After the children get used to the instructions, have them give each other commands.

Remember:

Bring the group together at the end of the activity and talk about the different roles, how their roles felt and what they did with their friends. Frog and Toad may then sit together for the next activity. After all, *Frog and Toad Are Friends* (another story about Frog and Toad).

GA1395

Frog and Toad Headbands

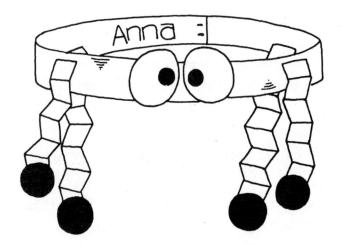

Use green construction paper for the frog headbands and brown for the toad headbands.

bands—2 1/2" (6.33 cm) wide strips long enough to go around the child's head. Add extra length to overlap and staple.

4 legs—two 1" x 9" (2.54 x 22.86 cm) strips accordion folded for back legs. two 1" x 7" (2.54 x 17.78 cm) strips accordion folded for the front legs.

4 feet— four black 2" (5.08 cm) squares

2 eyes—two white 2" x 3" (5.08 x 7.62 cm) rectangles two black 1" (2.54 cm) squares

Put the child's name on the back of the long strip.
Cut off the corners of the white triangles and black squares to round them off.
Glue the small black circles onto the white ovals.
Glue the larger black circles onto the legs.
Find the center of the headband by folding it in half.
Glue eyes close together on each side of the center.
Place the two shorter legs about 3" (7.62 cm) from the eyes.
Place the two longer legs behind each of the short legs.
Measure around the child's head.
Staple the headband.

GA1395

Frog and Toad

Connect each frog with a toad using a line.

Put matching hats on each pair.

Color the vests on each pair the same color.

Put matching boots on each pair.

Color the frogs green.

Color the toads brown.

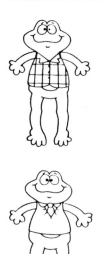

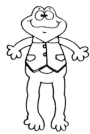

If you have time:

Turn your paper over. At the top of the paper, draw a toad and a frog that match.

At the bottom, make a list of things that these friends will do together.

Scarecrows

Mothers usually do not like piles of clothing strewn about the room. However, school is a bit different. While making these scarecrows, the clothing will be in the middle of the floor. Scarecrows are a real part of our past, and in some places are still used. However, most children have not helped make one. Today will be different.

Materials Needed:

1 set of adult clothing per group of children (hat, shoes, scarf, shirt, pants, mittens, belt, socks)

1 spinner per group of children (see next page)

task badges for each child, one set per group (see next page)

masking tape

bead necklaces of like colors per group, each group having a different color

Preparing for the Lesson:

Read *Hello, Mr. Scarecrow* by Rob Lewis (New York: Farrar, Straus, Giroux).

Before the children break into smaller groups, unpack the box, trunk or suitcase of clothes. Give each child one article and have him/her put it into a like pile.

Grouping the Children:

Children are divided into groups of four. Each child is given a bead necklace to denote the family group. The group finds a spot in the room and sits down. Each group has a spinner and three task cards.

Activity:

The children spin the spinner until someone gets the scarecrow. That person gets to be dressed as the scarecrow. All the children put their badges on with masking tape. The children who are not the scarecrow place the task cards face down and choose one.

Children take turns doing what their task cards state, spinning the spinner, selecting clothing from the pile or dressing the scarecrow.

Take pictures of the completed scarecrows and post them on a bulletin board. The children can also draw pictures of each scarecrow they make.

Since every child may want to be the scarecrow, let groups continue working until they have all had a chance, or give them another opportunity tomorrow.

Remember:

Bring the group together at the end of the activity and talk about the different tasks, how the jobs were all important and how they felt doing each job.

Scarecrow Task Cards and Spinner

Make a copy of the spinner and of each task card for each group of four children. Color the pictures. Mount them on lightweight cardboard. Laminate.

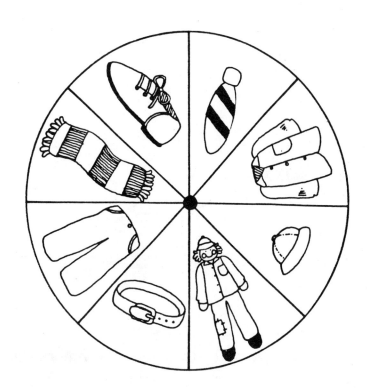

Dress the Scarecrow

Color the scarecrow.
Glue dried grass or straw on
the hands, feet and around the neck.
Choose a hat at the bottom of the page.
Color it. Cut it out and put it on your scarecrow.

If you have time:
Cut out patches of cloth to make your scarecrow more colorful.
On another sheet of blank paper, draw your scarecrow a friend. Color and
dress the friend to match.

Zookeepers

Feeding the animals is usually prohibited at the farm or zoo, but not in this classroom. Children work together in pairs to feed their animals, use their concepts of number to determine who has fed the animal more or less, and check the answers of each.

Materials Needed:

1 zoo animal picture per group (see next page)

paper plates, crayons and glue

5 red objects in Baggies for the Red Zookeeper

5 blue objects in Baggies for the Blue Zookeeper

bell

red bead necklaces for the Red Zookeeper, blue for Blue Zookeeper

Preparing for the Lesson:

Read *At the Zoo* by Eugene Booth (Raintree).

Prepare red and blue bead necklaces. Place the Baggies of "food" on a plate on the supply table. Have children cut out an animal, color it and glue it to a paper plate on the day before the lesson. Place these on the supply table as well.

Grouping the Children:

After reading the story, give half of the children red bead necklaces and half of them blue bead necklaces. Ask the Red Zookeepers to choose Blue Zookeepers for partners. Have children pass by the supply table in pairs to pick up red or blue food (to match their necklaces) and one animal for their group to feed. Have the children find a spot to sit and place their animal between them.

Teacher Directed Activity:

The teacher holds the bell and rings it the correct number of times as he/she reads each statement.

Teacher: Blue Zookeepers, feed your animal (ding, ding, ding) blue chips.

Group work: Have the Red Zookeeper count to make sure Blue is correct.

Teacher: Red Zookeepers, feed your animal (ding, ding) red chips.

Group work: Have the Blue Zookeeper count to make sure Red is correct.

Teacher: Zookeepers, how many chips did you feed your animal in all?

Group work: Let each Zookeeper count to make sure the other is correct.

Teacher: Zookeepers, who fed the animal the most chips?

Continue until the children tire of this. Let them work together in pairs to tell each other what to feed the animals.

Independent Activity:

After you are certain the children know how to do the activity, place the materials in a center. Let one child be the teacher and give the directions.

Remember:

Bring the group together at the end of the activity and talk about the different tasks, how their jobs were important and how they felt doing each job.

GA1395

Zoo Animals

Each of these animals belongs in the zoo. Color each animal.
Cut thin strips of black paper to make a cage for each.
Glue the cage over the animal.

Teacher: If you use this as a children's activity page, cut off the instructions below before copying the sheet.
For use with Zookeeper Cooperative Learning Activity
Directions for Teacher: Copy this page to make enough animals for each pair of children in your classroom. Roughly cut out the animals, not following the lines directly, and let each pair of children choose one. Have them color it as a team, cut it out and glue it to a paper plate.

I'm One of the Bunch

A bulletin board creates an opportunity for children to work together to show how each child is "one of the bunch." Working in pairs, the children construct their part of the bulletin board. Self-concept is built when children enjoy working together and seeing portraits of themselves displayed. A good book to read is *Will I Have a Friend?*

Materials Needed:

magic markers for each group of children

large sheet of white or pastel butcher paper cut into large puzzle pieces (The number of puzzle pieces should be the same number as classmates and teacher.)

Grouping the Children:

Have the children work together in groups of two or three.

Activity:

Have the children each choose a puzzle piece. The children draw portraits of the other children in their group to be placed on the "I'm One of the Bunch" bulletin board. Drawing each other develops interest in the uniqueness of each child.

Have children look at each other's name tags or desk tags and write the name of the child in the portrait at the bottom of the picture. Working on the floor or a very large table, children put their own portrait into the puzzle, assisting each other as needed. Display for open house or for self-concept and awareness unit.

Remember:

Review the process with the children.

I'm One of the Bunch

GA1395

I'm One of the Bunch

Color the children in this picture to look like children you know.

Glue the paper onto a piece of construction paper.

Let the paper dry overnight.

Turn the paper over to the construction paper side. Cut it into several pieces.

Do not look at the picture while you are cutting.

Turn all the pieces over and try to put your puzzle together.

18

GA1395

Draw a Friend

A great idea for Open House is to display life-size paper children sitting in the classroom seats when parents come to visit. Children work with a friend to draw and color each other.

Materials Needed:
large sheet of butcher paper
pencil
crayons or markers
large full-length mirror
small hand mirror

Preparing for the Lesson:
Using a model, point out body parts by name. Play games like Simon Says using body parts. Have children look at themselves in the mirror. Play a game with a friend to find out what color eyes, hair, skin, etc., the children have. How many legs, arms, eyes, etc., do you have?

Grouping the Children:
Children work in pairs.

Activity:
One child draws around his/her friend. They work together to draw, color and cut out the paper friend. Students switch tasks the next day. Now both friends are ready for Open House.

GA1395

What Things Go Together?

Friends go together.
What other things go together?
Draw lines to connect things that go together.
Color the pictures to show they go together.

If you have time:
Cut out the pictures. Glue them to small index cards. Put them with your friend's cards. Play Concentration.

GA1395

Leaf Search

In the fall, many trees lose their leaves. These become inexpensive materials for classroom use. Children can discover that leaves change colors and are of many different shapes. Children working together in groups of four match leaves that have the same shape. (For those in regions where leaves do not change, save leaves that are pruned from trees for this lesson.) Read *We Learn All About Fall* by Sharon MacDonald (D. S. Lake Publishers).

Materials Needed:
4 different shaped leaves per group
4 numbered tags (1 to 4) in a different color for each group
leaves of the same shape as above hidden in the classroom or a designated outdoor area

Grouping the Children:
Divide children into groups of four. Give each group a color name determined by the numbered tags that they receive. (Bead necklaces will help the younger ones.)

Preparing for the Lesson:
Show the children a pile of leaves. Pick them up one at a time and have the children tell you about the shapes. If a leaf is like one they have seen before, let the children put it into a pile with its match. After the demonstration, give each group one leaf per child. Label the leaves with numbered tags.

Directions:
Children work together to help group members find matching leaves in the room or designated outdoor area. The members of the group examine Leaf #1 and all begin to search. When Leaf #1 has been found, all must agree that its shape matches the sample. The search resumes for Leaf #2, etc. After all four leaves have been found, students share the leaves to make leaf rubbings. When the rubbings are done, children label the pictures of the leaves with the numbers 1, 2, 3 or 4.

Remember:
Talk with the children about the difficulties they had finding leaves and how they helped one another look for just the right leaf.

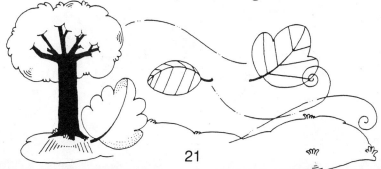

GA1395

Leaf Search

Below are leaves of many shapes and sizes.
Find pairs that match.
Draw a line to connect them.
Color them so they look the same.

If you have time:

Cut out the leaves. Mount each on a 3" x 3" (7.62 x 7.62 cm) sheet of black construction paper. Put your initials on the back of each square of paper. Mix them all up and match the leaves again. Mix your pile with a friend and find matches for them all.

GA1395

Little Pumpkins

Mini cheese balls that look like little pumpkins are nutritious and tasty treats to make and eat. Children work in an assembly line of three to make cheese balls.

Materials Needed:

1" (2.54 cm) cube of cream cheese
1 tablespoon of grated yellow cheese on a plastic butter lid
whole crackers
1 tablespoon of cracker crumbs in a Baggie
3 plastic knives
task cards mounted on different colored paper for each group (cream cheese, grated cheese, cracker crumbs)

Preparing for the Lesson:

Put all the materials on trays for each group with the task cards upside down. Make sure that all children wash their hands with soap and water before the lesson. Read *Pumpkin, Pumpkin* by J. Titherington (Greenwillow).

Grouping the Children:

Three children are in each assembly line. Each child will select a task card which is upside down on the tray.

Directions:

Demonstrate each of the tasks. (1) Roll the cube of cream cheese into a ball on a piece of waxed paper. (2) Roll the cream cheese ball in the grated cheese.
(3) Shake the cream cheese ball in the Baggie of cracker crumbs.

Set the children up in groups of three along the edges of the tables. Put a tray at the end where the cheese balls will be placed.

Children spread the cheese balls onto crackers and enjoy as a snack.

Remember:

Review the procedures with the children to see what problems they had.

Additional Cooperative Learning Activity:

On the day before the lesson, set up groups of three to get the materials for the cheese balls. One gets a small brick of cream cheese and a table knife to cut cubes of cream cheese. One gets a grater and cheddar cheese. One gets a rolling pin and crackers to crush. (Do it inside an unlocked Baggie to control the mess.)

Task Cards

Directions to the teacher:

Copy this sheet, one set of cards for each group.

Mount each sheet on a different color of construction paper.

Cut them out and laminate them.

cream cheese

grated cheese

cracker crumbs

24

GA1395

Little Pumpkins to Eat

Color each of the pictures.
Cut the pictures out.
Put the pictures in order on a strip of 4 1/2" x 18" (11.41 x 45.72 cm) construction paper.
Write the name of your friend under the picture to show what he/she did.
Write your name under the picture of the task you did.

GA1395

Mr. Bear Says

Children can play Simon Says with their paper bears as they review their shapes and learn words of location (inside, under, next to, etc.). Read *The Spooky Old Tree* by Stan and Jan Berenstain (Random House) to introduce the lesson.

Materials Needed:
1 small container per group
1 paper bear per child (see next page)
1 shape symbol per child

Preparing for the Lesson:
Each child is given a paper bear to cut out and a shape to glue on its tummy.

Grouping the Children:
Children work in pairs or small groups with at least one higher functioning child and one lower functioning child per group.

Directed Activity:
The teacher gives directions to the children as they begin their task.
Teacher: Mr. Bear says, "Put the Circle Bear on top of the box."
Teacher: Mr. Bear says, "Put the Triangle Bear inside the box."
Teacher: Mr. Bear says, "Put the Circle Bear under the box."
Teacher: Mr. Bear says, "Put the Triangle Bear next to the box."
Teacher: Mr. Bear says, "Put all the bears in front of the box."

Activity:
Children can give each other directions and check each other. As their skill increases, increase the number of people and bears per group of children and give them different shapes.

Remember:
Review with the children what fun they had working in pairs and checking each other's work. See if they think they were helpful to each other.

GA1395

Mr. Bear Says

Color the bear.
Cut it out.
Glue a shape on its belly.

27

GA1395

Name _____

Mr. Bear Says

Mr. Bear says, "Find bears with matching shapes on their bellies."
Mr. Bear says, "Draw lines to connect the matching bears."
Mr. Bear says, "Color the matching bears the same."

GA1395

Shape Detectives (Jigsaw)

Shape hunts are great fun for young children. They see shapes in things that we have grown to ignore. In this activity students hunt in groups of three to become aware of the many things around them that are made of basic geometric shapes. Have shape crackers for a reward after the hunt.

Materials Needed:

Students in a group will wear badges of the same color.

Each student in a group receives three shape cards (three squares, three circles or three triangles) that are of the same color as his/her badge.

The badge is a matching color and is of a different shape.

Grouping the Children:

Students will work together in groups of three selected by the teacher. They wear badges to denote their groups.

Preparing for the Lesson:

Introduce shapes one at a time using a collection of objects of different sizes. Compare and contrast the shapes and articles. Place three shapes in front of the children and play What's Missing? Read *The Shape of Me and Other Stuff* by Dr. Seuss (Random House).

Activity:

One child in each group has three circle cards, another has three square cards, etc. Children leave their groups and regroup with shape counterparts.

All circle detectives work together in a search through the room for objects that are shaped like a circle. Square detectives work together, and triangle detectives work together. They take turns taping their shape cards on or near an object which matches the shape. When all of the shape cards have been distributed in the room, the detectives return to their original group of children.

Shape detectives stay in their color group. The circle detective shows his/her group the objects that are circles. The square detective shows his/her group the objects that are squares. Each shape detective shares his/her findings with group members.

Remember:

Review the process and have children tell you things they found of various shapes. Monitor while children work.

GA1395

Play Shape Detective

Color all of the ▭ blue.

Color all of the △ red.

Color all of the ◯ yellow.

Color all of the ▢ green.

Ghosts and Bats

Halloween has its ghosts and bats, but how many children can practice counting, checking and writing skills using lima beans that have been transformed into bats and ghosts?

Materials Needed:

10 large lima beans painted black with silver eyes on one side and painted white with a face on the other side

shaker (cup/lid from laundry detergent bottle or a paper or plastic cup)

number work sheet for beginning writers

pencil

pumpkin-shaped house cut from 12" x 9" (30.48 x 22.86 cm) piece of felt

Preparing for the Lesson:

Counting and writing activities for the numbers 0 to 5 precede this activity.

Grouping the Children:

Organize children in groups of three. Tasks are shaker, counter and writer. Distribute materials and tasks in the following manner.

The student who is the shaker receives the cup/lid and five (or ten) bat/ghost bean manipulatives. His/Her task is shaking the beans, dumping them onto the pumpkin house and checking the counter.

The counter receives the pumpkin house, counts the number of bats and ghosts that are face up after being dumped and checks the writer.

The writer receives the work sheet and pencil and the task of tracing the numeral that corresponds with the number of bats or ghosts counted.

Activity:

The shaker starts the process by shaking the beans and dumping them onto the felt house. The counter counts ghosts and bats (older children can count ghosts and bats and write equations.) The counter tells the writer the answer. All check one another. When the writer is finished, the children begin again. Children retrace numerals when a whole column has been traced. Rotate tasks to allow all children to experience each type of activity.

Remember:

Talk about this experience in terms of which was the favorite job and why, how they liked it and other ways to do it.

GA1395

Ghosts and Bats

Count the ghosts in the large boxes.
Put the number in the small boxes.

Count the bats in the large boxes.
Put the number in the small boxes.

If you have time:
Color the bats black. Color the ghosts white. Cut out the boxes of ghosts and bats. Put the ghosts in numerical order. Put the bats in numerical order. Glue each set to a separate long strip of cash register paper.

     GA1395

Native American Beads

During the early settlement of the United States, the Native Americans traded handmade articles such as beaded garments or necklaces for supplies that they needed. To show how these necklaces were made and to let children see how it feels to trade, try making and trading Native American Beads.

Materials Needed:
   pasta shapes that can be strung
   rubbing alcohol
   food coloring
   1 piece of yarn 24" (60.96 cm) long for each child

Preparing for the Lesson:
   To dye pasta, pour two cups of pasta into a plastic reclosable bag; add one tablespoon of alcohol and several drops of food coloring. Close the bag and shake. Dump the pasta onto a newspaper to dry. To make the yarn easy to string, dip the ends of yarn into glue and allow to dry on waxed paper.

Grouping the Children:
   Group the children in sets of three.

Directions:
   Talk with the children about how the people who met the Native Americans traded for the jewels and valuables that they had. Read *Columbus* by I. & E. D'Aulaire (Doubleday). Demonstrate how to make a pasta pattern using three colors. Give each group of children three strings. Each child selects one color of pasta to string. Each child strings only the color of pasta that he/she has. The children must take turns passing the string and stringing pieces of pasta of different colors to make an ABC pattern. Tie the ends to make necklaces. Make three necklaces, working on only one at a time. When finished, children can trade their necklaces with someone else.

Remember:
   Monitor the children as they work, and ask them to show you their patterns. When everyone is finished, ask each person to notice the patterns in the other children's necklaces. Chat with them about working together.

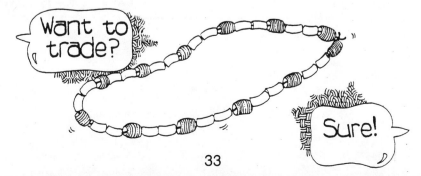

GA1395

Stringing Beads

Below are three strings of beads.
Place the necklace you made near one of the strings.
Color your pattern on one of the strings.
Borrow your friend's necklace.
Color your friend's pattern on the next string.
Borrow your other friend's necklace.
Color this friend's pattern in the last string.
Write names next to each of the strings.

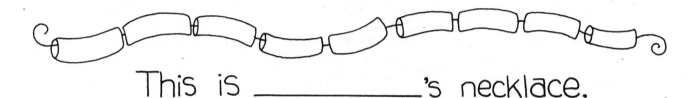

This is _____'s necklace.

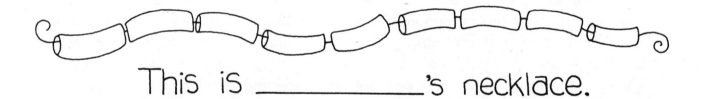

This is _____'s necklace.

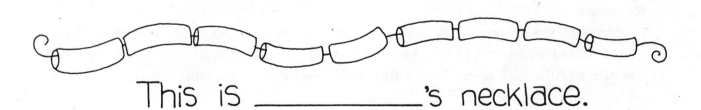

This is _____'s necklace.

GA1395

How Does Your Garden Grow?

"Just how does your garden grow?" is the question asked of Mistress Mary. Most gardeners use shovels, hoes and watering cans, but not these special gardeners. Children work together in pairs to arrange their gardens of vegetable prints using the concept of patterns.

Materials Needed:

 vegetables or fruits cut in half
 thick tempera paint in shallow containers
 3' (.91 m) adding machine tape
 masking tape
 newspaper to cover the table
 paint shirts

Preparing for the Lesson:

During a teacher-directed activity, develop the concept of patterns using real objects, sounds or actions. Read *The Tiny Seed* by E. Carle (Picture Book Studio) to talk about how plants really grow.

Grouping the Children:

Group the children in pairs.

Directions:

Each child will print with one vegetable and one color. The pair of children must take turns to make a specific pattern. An AB pattern would be the simplest to start. More complex patterns (AABB) may be possible after the first strip is complete. Ask two groups to get together to make an even more complicated pattern (ABCD or AABCCD, etc.) The strips of vegetable print patterns may be used as bulletin board borders or as headbands.

Remember:

Monitor the children as they work. Talk with them about their patterns. Have them say the pattern as they print.

Group the children together at the end of the painting and have them share their prints with you.

GA1395

What Pattern Can You Make?

Color the patterns below.
Write the name of the pattern in the box.

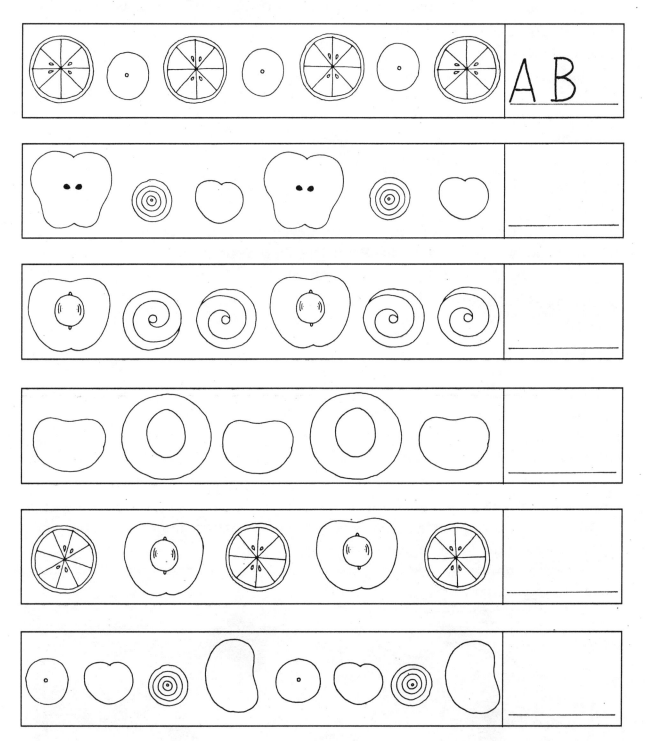

If you have time:
Take a sheet of blank paper. Fold it into several boxes. Draw one fruit in some of the boxes. Draw another fruit in the other boxes. Cut them out. Arrange them in a pattern.

36

GA1395

Five Kernels of Corn

A long time ago the Pilgrims gave thanks for a new land, home, food, freedom and their families. Some Pilgrims gave each member of their family five kernels of corn and each shared five reasons for being thankful. Children working in groups of three use thinking skills to share five reasons why they are thankful today.

Materials Needed:

5 kernels of candy corn per person
small bowl
crayons or magic markers
2 sheets of paper for each child
butcher paper for accordion book
glue

Preparing for the Lesson:

Read and discuss *Squanto and the First Thanksgiving* by J. Kessel (Carolrhoda Books).

Discuss being thankful.

Grouping the Children:

The children will work in groups of three.

Directions:

Give each group a small bowl with fifteen kernels of corn in it. When they get to their sharing spot, each child counts out his/her own five kernels of corn.

Children then take turns sharing a reason to be thankful and placing a kernel of corn into the small bowl. After they all have shared five reasons to be thankful, they work together to make an accordion book to show others some of their reasons for being thankful. Each child draws two pictures to glue into the accordion book. The books are shared with other groups.

Remember:

Bring the total group together to review the process. Post the Thankful Books in the room for others to view.

GA1395

Name _____

Five Things I'm Thankful For

A long time ago the Pilgrims gave thanks for a new land, home, food, freedom and their families. Some Pilgrims gave each member of their family five kernels of corn and each shared five reasons for being thankful.

Draw one thing you are thankful for on each of the kernels below. Write about each of them on the back of this paper.

38

Do You Like My Hat?

November is a fine time to talk about hats. As we discuss Pilgrims and Native Americans, we talk about hats. When the weather gets colder we talk about other types of hats. Hats have many purposes. Children will work together in this cooperative learning activity to make Hat Books by drawing hats for workers, special occasions and for protection.

Materials Needed:

9" x 9" (22.86 x 22.86 cm) tagboard with picture of head per group
5" x 9" (12.7 x 22.86 cm) paper for each child in group
markers
staplers

Preparing for the Lesson:

Have a Hat Day where each child brings a special hat from home, one of their own or one belonging to a family member. Be sure they tell about how the hat is used, when and why. Read *A Three Hat Day* by L. Geringer or *Jennie's Hat* by Ezra Jack Keats.

Grouping the Children:

The children will work in groups of six to draw a hat to put in the Hat Book. The hats are drawn on 5" x 9" (12.7 x 22.86 cm) sheets of paper. The teacher will need to assist in the assembly of the books. All hats are stacked on top of one another and stapled on the left side of the tagboard. The top hat looks as if it were on the head. When it is turned, another hat comes into view.

To form a table of contents, the illustrators and authors should write their names on the first page of the book beside the number indicating the placement of their hats. Children can write or dictate about their hats. The Hat Books can be placed in the reading corner or borrowed to share at home.

Remember:

Chat with the children about how you put the book together while you are doing it. Let them tell you about having helped make it.

Have each group of children share their book with another group.

GA1395

How Many Scoops?

Dyed rice in holiday colors is an inexpensive material to use when teaching the concept of volume. Young children should begin estimating and thinking about why a container should hold more scoops. Hands-on activities help children learn to estimate through discovery.

Materials Needed:

orange rice	masking tape	scoop
yellow rice	magic marker	funnel
star stickers	table knife	cup for scoop

3 clear plastic containers of different shapes per group

Rice is easy to dye. Pour about 2 cups (480 ml) of rice into a reclosable plastic bag, add one tablespoon of alcohol and several drops of food coloring. Close the bag and shake until rice is colored. Pour onto newspapers to dry.

Preparing for the Lesson:

Demonstrate how to fill a measuring cup, level it with a table knife and fill a container using a funnel. Alternate colors of rice so the number of scoops can be easily counted. Before beginning, have children predict how many scoops will fill the container. Record guesses on the container. Count scoops while filling the container and again after it is filled. Compare guesses.

Grouping the Children:

Assign the children to work in pairs.

Activity:

One child gets a container of yellow rice, and one gets orange rice. They first predict which of the three containers will hold more scoops and tell why. Each child will label the predicted container with masking tape and his/her name.

One child pours one scoop into the first container, and then the other child pours a scoop into the second container. They count the scoops as they fill all three containers.

When finished filling, children put a star sticker on the one that holds the most scoops.

Remember:

During closure activities, have children tell about their discoveries. Have them discuss their discoveries.

GA1395

How Many Scoops?

In each of the boxes below is a jar with lines on it.

Each of the lines represents one scoop of colored rice.

Start at the bottom of each jar and draw in colored rice.

Fill each jar as full as you wish.

Count the scoops and put the number in the box.

Ask a friend to check to see if you counted the scoops correctly.

GA1395

Wrapping It Up!

Wrapping a gift for someone can be as exciting to a child as choosing the gift itself. In this activity, children work in pairs to wrap gifts for family members or pals from another class.

Materials Needed:
gift in a box
wrapping paper
ribbon or bows
tape
scissors

Preparing for the Lesson:
Children can make their own wrapping paper using the printing suggested in How Does Your Garden Grow, page 35. Children can use sponges painted with holiday symbols and make patterns on white tissue paper.

During circle time, gift wrapping is demonstrated by the teacher and a child. The package is place in the center of the paper. One edge is folded over. The child holds the paper in place while the teacher places tape on the paper to hold it to the gift.

The opposite edge is folded over. The child again holds the paper in place while the teacher places the tape on the paper to hold it to the first paper.

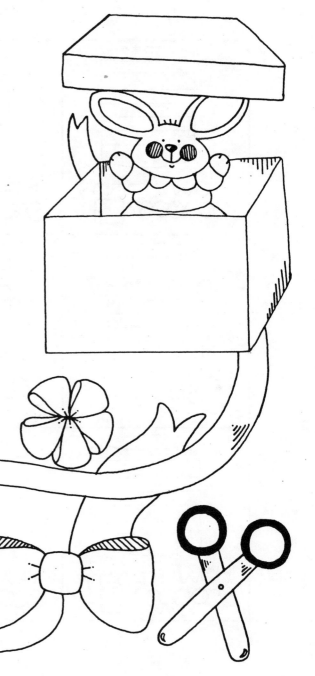

GA1395

The two corners of one end are folded down to the gift. The tip made by these folds is folded down on top of the package. The child holds this while the teacher tapes the tip to the package.

The other end is done the same way. Older children can tie the string around and use curling ribbon to tie a bow to the front.

Grouping the Children:

Children work in pairs chosen by the teacher or by themselves.

Directions:

Each child has a gift to wrap. The partner acts as assistant to the child who is wrapping the gift.

Remember:

When the children are finished, have them tell you about how the process worked, what problems they had, how they solved them together and which was the hardest thing to do.

Wrapping It Up!

Color the packages and bows to match.
Cut out the bows.
Glue the bows to the correct packages.

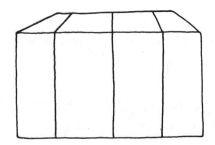

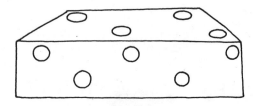

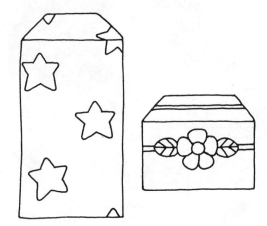

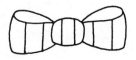

GA1395

Tree Trimmers

During the holiday time, children love to make things for their own tree or gifts for other people. This activity requires that the children work together in an assembly line of four to make tree ornaments or decorated wooden pins for the holidays.

Materials Needed:

wooden cutout (tree, valentine, butterfly, etc.)
thick craft glue
string to hang ornament or a pin back
small buttons
newspaper
spray paint (optional)

Preparing for the Lesson:

Make three ahead of time to show the children. One has a string. One has a pin back. One has been sprayed gold or silver when completed.

Demonstrate careful gluing of buttons onto the surface of the wooden cutout.

Grouping the Children:

Children work in groups of four.

Directions:

Children sit in a circle of four on the floor. Place a piece of newspaper on the floor in the middle of them. Each child glues one button onto the wood surface and passes it to the next person in the circle. Continue until the surface is covered by gluing the buttons close to each other. Continue with at least three additional wooden cutouts so that each child has one.

Have the children make extras to use as gifts.

Children can use the decorations on the class or school tree, take them home as gifts or for their own tree or give them to support personnel in the building. Let the children wrap these gifts using the process in Wrapping It Up! p. 42.

Remember:

Talk about the process, the problems and the pleasures.

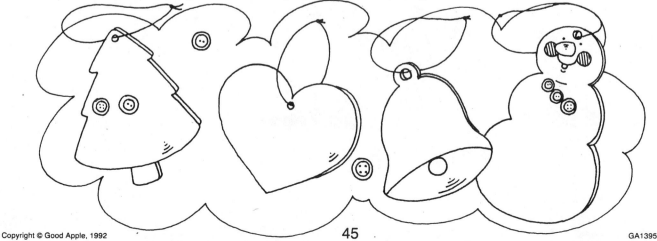

Name _____

Tree Trimmer

Color each of the trees green before you start decorating.
Color all of the ornaments before you start decorating the trees.
Your teacher will tell you a number (0 to 10) to put on each bucket.
Cut out the correct number of ornaments at the bottom.
Glue them to the tree.
How many ornaments did you have left over?_____

Copyright © Good Apple, 1992   GA1395

Stocking Stuffers

Refrigerator magnets are great gifts to give parents or grandparents. Children work together in assembly lines to make puppy dog magnets using Milk-Bone dog biscuits.

Materials Needed:

1 large Milk-Bone dog biscuit
2 medium wiggly eyes (glue-on type)
1 black pompon
1 1/2" (3.79 cm) magnetic strip
small red bow
2 brown or black felt ears (tear drop shaped)
red felt tongue
Styrofoam meat tray or paper plate for each dog bone

Preparing for the Lesson:

Demonstrate each job on the assembly line. Emphasis should be on gluing techniques. Provide hand wipes for each assembly line if children should need to clean their hands. (The teacher has previously sprayed the Milk-Bones with a fixative and glued a magnetic strip to the back of each biscuit. Each Milk-Bone is placed on a meat tray.)

Grouping the Children:

Assign jobs to each child. Five children are needed for each assembly line.
Job #1 - Glue two eyes.
Job #2 - Glue nose.
Job #3 - Glue red bow at top of head.
Job #4 - Glue tongue.
Job #5 - Glue ears.

Remember:

Watch the children as they work and compliment them on working well together. Have them review the process with you when the activity is completed.

GA1395

How Did It Happen?

Below are six dog bones.

Each bone has a number under it to tell you which one was first, which was second and so on.

The first one should have nothing on it.

The second one will have only two eyes.

The third one should have two eyes and a round nose.

Can you finish the others?

When you have drawn all of the features, color the bones.

If you have time:

Cut out each of the bones and put them on a long strip (4 1/2" x 18") (11.41 x 45.72 cm) of construction paper. Be sure to put your name on the back of the paper.

GA1395

Puzzle Partners

There are many holiday puzzles available which have 24 pieces or fewer for young children. For children a bit older, try the ones with 48 or 100 pieces. Get one puzzle for each group of children. Groups for this activity can vary from two to four. This activity can be used any time throughout the year.

Materials Needed:

gift box with a hole in side
1 puzzle

Grouping the Children:

Children will work in twos, threes or fours.

Directions:

Children will take turns removing a puzzle piece from the gift box without looking. (Help children by telling them to feel the puzzle pieces and try to get a piece with a straight edge first.) Each time a puzzle piece is removed, the child tries to fit it to the puzzle. If it will not fit, keep the puzzle piece until it will fit.

Remember:

Chat with them about how they liked doing the puzzle in a group.

GA1395

Christmas Bear
Color by Number

1 = brown   2=red   3=green   4=yellow   5=blue   6=black

GA1395

The Night Before Christmas

On the night before Christmas, Santa is still at the North Pole sorting toys. More elves are needed to help Santa sort stuffed toys that are spotted, striped and plain. Read Walt Disney's *Santa's Toy Shop* (Golden Press).

Materials Needed:

Santa's Bag work sheets, pages 52-54

toy work sheet, page 55

scissors

glue

green elf headbands, page 56

Preparing for the Lesson:

During circle time, discuss and show items that are spotted, striped and plain. Use wrapping paper, fabric, pictures and stuffed animals. For a more involved project, sew simple drawstring bags of plain, spotted and striped material to put these things in. Involve children in sorting these items.

Grouping the Children:

Children will work in groups of three. Each is given a different Santa's Bag work sheet and a sheet of animals. Working together they look for items that fit the classifications.

Children find a picture from the work sheet, cut it out and give it to their friend with the correct bag. Children must agree that it belongs in the bag. Children cannot glue their own pictures onto their own bags.

Follow-up Center:

Put demonstration materials in a center for sorting. Suggest that children explore at home for other objects.

Remember:

Chat with children about the sorting job they have just done. See how they liked working together.

GA1395

Santa Bag

Color your Santa Bag.
Sit with your friends.
Cut out animals that match their bags.
Give them to your friends.
When you get animals from your friends, glue them onto your bag.

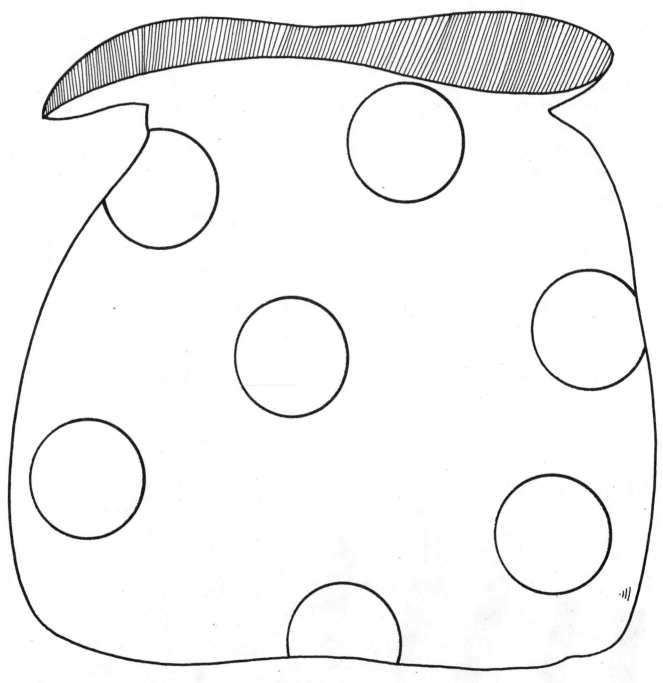

How many spotted animals do you have?_____
How many striped animals does your friend have?_____
How many plain animals does your friend have? _____
Who has the most?_____

Santa Bag

Color your Santa Bag.
Sit with your friends.
Cut out animals that match their bags.
Give them to your friends.
When you get animals from your friends, glue them onto your bag.

How many striped animals do you have?_____
How many spotted animals does your friend have?_____
How many plain animals does your friend have? _____
Who has the most?_____

Santa Bag

Color your Santa Bag.

Sit with your friends.

Cut out animals that match their bags.

Give them to your friends.

When you get animals from your friends, glue them onto your bag.

How many plain animals do you have?_____

How many striped animals does your friend have?_____

How many spotted animals does your friend have? _____

Who has the most?_____

GA1395

The Night Before Christmas

Find animals that match your friends' bags.
Cut them out.
Give them to your friends and keep your own.
Glue yours onto your bag.

 GA1395

Elf Headbands

Make headbands out of separate colors of paper.
Each child in the classroom gets one elf.
Children form groups of three.

GA1395

Building a Snowperson

Usually about the time real snow is needed for a school project, there is no snow! Children working together in threes use thinking skills to create a snowperson using only a few pieces of paper and a bottle of glue. You might read *Frosty the Snowman*, but don't show pictures.

Materials Needed:

small scraps of paper in various colors
large sheet of white paper
glue

Preparing for the Lesson:

Give each group glue, white paper and colored paper scraps.

Grouping the Children:

Children are grouped in threes.

Directions:

Explain that the objective is to make a snowperson using only the materials given. Instruct the children to talk about how these materials could be made into a snowperson. After sharing ideas, construction may begin with all children in the group working together.

Remember:

Finished products are shared with the whole class at circle time. Discuss how the children felt when given the task. Did they think they could make a snowperson without snow?

GA1395

Name _____

Snowperson

Look at the snowperson.
Make this snowperson look like the one you made with your friends.

Animals on Parade

Learning to recognize and make patterns is a necessary part of young children's math development. Working together children can make Animals on Parade. A good book to read is *Millions of Cats* by W. Gag (Scholastic) or *The Friendly Book* by M. W. Brown (A Little Golden Book).

Materials Needed:

3' (.91 m) adding machine tape for each child
crayons

Preparing for the Lesson:

During circle time, demonstrate A B C D patterns with real objects.

Grouping the Children:

Children are grouped in fours.

Directions:

Have each child in the group pick an animal that he/she can draw well. Draw that animal on the far left end of the adding machine tape facing the left. Pass the sheet to a friend on the left. When everyone has passed the sheets, the next child draws the animal that he/she has chosen. The group continues to pass the paper and draw until the tape is full. Younger children can use animal stamps and form an assembly line.

Remember:

Get the children together to share their Animals on Parade. Post them in the hall for everyone to see.

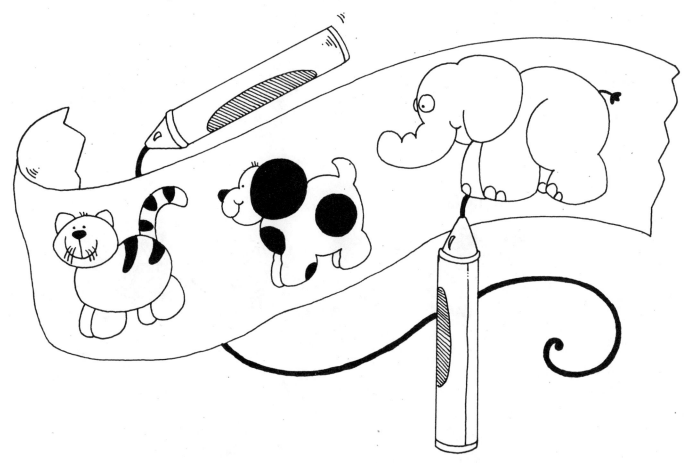

What's the Pattern?

Color the boxcars to make a pattern.
What pattern did you make?_____ _____ . _____ _____

Color the cars to make a pattern.
What pattern did you make?_____ _____ _____ _____

Color the stars to make a pattern.
What pattern did you make?_____ _____ _____ _____

Color the dogs to make a pattern.
What pattern did you make?_____ _____ _____ _____

If you have time:
After your teacher or friend has checked your paper, cut out the objects above and rearrange them to make different sets of patterns. Name each.

GA1395

Monsters Eat Junk

Sorting objects by color, size, texture and shape can be fun when the items are fed to a monster made by the children. Working in pairs, children sort objects from a junk drawer.

Materials Needed:

junk drawer (box) per group
variety of miscellaneous junk
monster made by each pair of children from milk carton, buttons, fake hair, etc.

Preparing for the Lesson:

Children work in pairs to create a monster that eats junk.

Directions:

Children work in pairs to find the following things as the teacher shows an example. Children take turns selecting junk objects and checking each other's decisions. The children feed the chosen objects to the monster. The teacher directs the children to find all the things shaped like triangles, things that are red, things that are soft, things made out of plastic, things that are small, things with holes, etc. Once they get the idea, children can give their partners directions.

Remember:

Review the fun the children had with the monsters after they finish and get tired of finding junk.

Feed us- We're hungry!

Name_____

The J Monster

The J Monster only eats things that start with *J*.
Color all the things that start with *J*.
Cut out all the things that start with *J*.
Glue these things to the J Monster.

62

GA1395

Clown for a Day

Children love to take pictures with a real camera, especially on Clown Day. Clown Day happens when children come to school dressed as clowns, culminating a unit on the circus or on clowns. A great way to record the day for others to see is to make a hall bulletin board constructed by the children and the teacher.

Materials Needed:

6" (15.24 cm) of oaktag circle pattern   film
scissors   rubber cement
pencil   black marker
camera (instant)   parent letter (see next page)
2 sheets construction paper 6" x 6" (15.24 x 15.24 cm)

Grouping the Children:

Each pair of children, dressed as clowns, works together to make two circles to be placed on the bulletin board to represent balls being juggled by a clown.

Activity:

The children help each other draw around the pattern to make two circles, one for a picture and one for a drawing. Each child then cuts out the two circles.

Partners take pictures of each other using an instant picture camera. Children carefully glue their pictures onto the circles, write their names with a marker and place it on the bulletin board.

While waiting for their turn with the camera, children draw portraits of their partners faces on their other circle.

Remember:

Ask children how they helped each other and how they felt doing it.

Bulletin Board:

Clown for a Day

To: _____ (Parents)

From: _____ (Teacher)

ANNOUNCING!
CLOWN DAY

Who: Your Child

What and Where: Come to school dressed like a clown

When:

Clown Day is a special day to enjoy learning activities using clowns as the theme. Activities at school may include math, science, reading, art, music, cooking, face painting and coordination. Suggestions for a clown costume are an old or funny hat, baggy shirt, etc. Children should look similar to a hobo clown.

Thank you for your help in getting your child ready for Clown Day.

GA1395

Where's My Partner?

Look carefully at each of the clown faces below.
Find the pairs that match.
Color them so that they are the same.

If you have time:
Cut out the clown faces. Glue them in pairs to a 6" x 18" (15.24 x 45.72 cm)
strip of construction paper.

Polka-Dot Clown

Polka dots and clowns go together. Polka-Dot Clown has movable/removable spots that are used to make a graph. Children manipulate real objects and then transfer those findings to make a bar graph. Manipulatives are re-used to make this a self-checking activity.

Materials Needed:

1 clown work sheet for each group
container of about 20 soda bottle caps sprayed five different colors (plastic game markers would do) (Give each group no more than five of each color.)
crayons of the same color as bottle caps
1 blank graph

Preparing for the Lesson:

Whole-group activities in graphing have been presented and children have an understanding of graphing and making bar graphs.

Grouping the Children:

Children will work in pairs.

Activity:

Children place each bottle cap on the clown's costume on the clown work sheet (see page 67). When all caps have been placed, children take turns tracing around a cap and coloring in the spot it leaves on the clown work sheet. As they remove the bottle cap, they place it on a graph (see page 68), putting like caps in columns or rows.

When all caps have been placed on the graph, children take turns coloring in each space with its corresponding color on the graph work sheet.

After work is completed, children can check their work by placing caps back on either work sheet to see if there is a match.

Let children compare the completed graphs in a whole-group activity.

Remember:

Chat with the children as they work asking how they're getting along, who's responsible for what, how they like their jobs.

GA1395

Decorate the Clown

Take turns with your partner to put dots on this clown.

67

Graph the Clown's Polka Dots

GA1395

Digging Up Good Snacks

Care of teeth and nutrition are concepts taught during Dental Health Week to help children become better decision makers in "digging up good snacks." Children work together using their understanding of dental health and nutrition to select healthy foods for snacks.

Materials Needed:

food pictures mounted on 3" x 5" (7.62 x 12.7 cm) cards
picture of a happy tooth and a sad tooth (see next page)
healthy snack

Preparing for the Lesson:

About two weeks before this lesson, do the following experiment. Explain that an egg shell is very similar to a tooth. Put an egg shell into a jar of water and another egg shell into a jar of soda pop. Ask children to predict what will happen to the egg shells. Write predictions that children make.

During circle time, discuss the results of the experiment. Discuss with the children other foods high in sugar.

Hide good snacks for the children (small apples, a small bag of carrot sticks, cheese sticks or cereal mixture or a small box of raisins) in large containers of unpopped corn or rice.

Grouping the Children:

Group the children in pairs. Give each pair a happy and sad tooth and a set of food cards.

Directions:

Each child in the pair will draw a card, determine whether it is a good or bad snack, check the response with his or her partner and place the card on the happy or sad tooth. When all the groups are finished, children share how they solved their problem.

After the lesson, each child "digs up a snack" in the larger container of unpopped popcorn or uncooked rice.

Remember:

Chat with the children about this activity as they brush their teeth or have snacks each day for the next week.

GA1395

Is This Tooth Happy or Sad?

Decide whether you want this tooth to be happy or sad.
Draw a face on it.
Cut out pictures that make this tooth happy or sad.
Glue them onto the tooth.

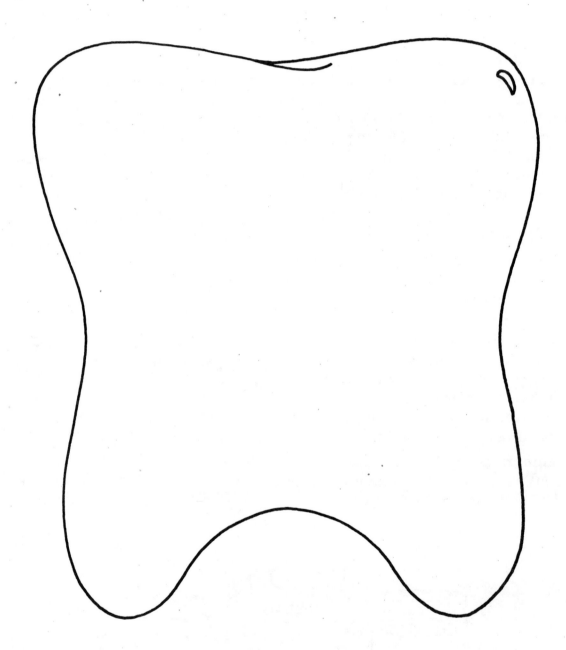

If you have time:
Cut out the molar. Trace around it on a sheet of white paper. Cut out the second tooth. Staple the edges together except at the top. Stuff the tooth with newspaper or tissue paper. Staple closed. Hang up in your room.

GA1395

What's Good? What's Not?

Color all the foods on this page.

If it is good for you and your teeth, draw a big happy face on it.

If it is bad for you and your teeth, draw a big circle around it and "X" it out.

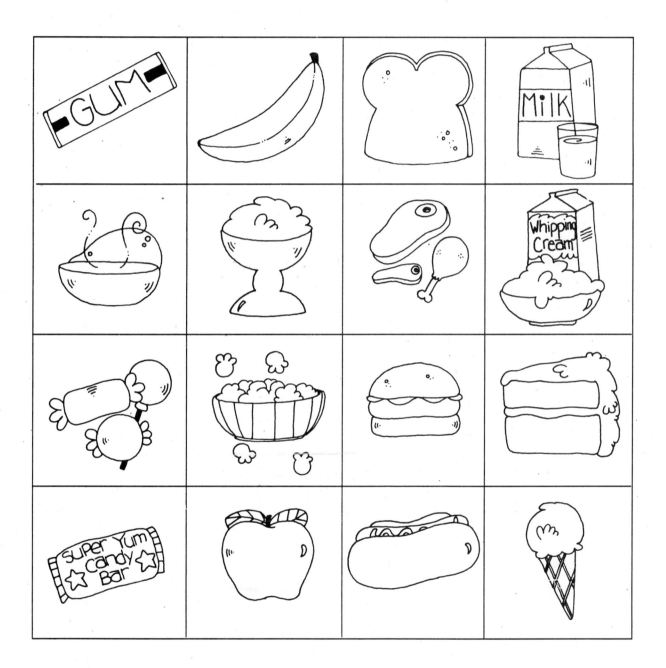

GA1395

Monsters Everywhere

Things that go bump in the night cause children to imagine monsters in the closet and under the bed. Children working together in groups of six or seven create a monster book. A good book to read is *Is There a Monster in My Closet?*

Materials Needed:
sheet of paper per child
markers or crayons or watercolors
book cover
scissors

Preparing for the Lesson:
On the back of the paper, print horizontal dotted lines 1/3 and 2/3 of the distance from the top.

Grouping the Children:
Divide the class into equal groups of about six or seven children.

Directions:
Each child will draw a monster on a sheet of paper. After the pictures of monsters are assembled by each group inside a book cover, each child carefully cuts on the dotted lines on the back of his or her monster. The divided pages of the book may be turned to create many versions of monsters.

Remember:
Have the children share their books with the other children. Place them in the reading center for all to enjoy. As they work, encourage them to talk about what frightens them.

GA1395

Night Noises

Many things happen at night.
Many things happen in the day.
Color the skies in these pictures the right color.
Black is for night.
Blue is for day.

If you have time:
Cut out the boxes with the pictures. Glue the night pictures to one half of a piece of 9" x 12" (22.86 x 30.48 cm) black construction paper. Glue the day pictures to one half of a piece of 9" x 12" (22.86 x 30. 48 cm) blue construction paper. Look in magazines for day and night pictures. Cut them out and glue them to the correct piece of paper.

Scrambled Eggs

Making a sensory memory game for the children in the classroom is the object of this activity. Children work in pairs to make two eggs for the game called Scrambled Eggs.

Materials Needed:

1 folded egg-shape per child (construction paper)
sensory material (sand, cotton balls, fabric, wallpaper, sandpaper, foil, etc.)
scissors
glue
newspaper to cover tabletop
small spoon for measuring
container or box for storage

Grouping the Children:

Children work in pairs at a table.

Directions:

Each child glues a sensory material such as one spoonful of sand or a square of foil, etc., onto one-half of a construction paper egg. The remaining half of the egg is prepared by the partner using the same material. Each pair of children makes two eggs.

When the two eggs have been completed, each is cut in half. The eggs are placed in the game center.

When children are ready to play, the eggs are placed upside down on the table or floor and Concentration rules are followed. Children may play in groups of four.

Remember:

Check to see how the children enjoyed working together to make the eggs and again to see how they liked playing with their own made materials.

GA1395

Find the Match

The eggs at the bottom of this page have lost their other half.
The other half is along the right-hand side of the page.
Color the matches the same to show that they match.
Cut off the right-hand side and the bottom where the eggs are.
Glue them onto the basket.

R * O * B * O * T

All generations are fascinated with robots. A tiny amount of imagination and a pretend robot set the foundation for a reading readiness activity that can be extended at home.

Materials Needed:

    1 milk carton robot for each two children (see next page for directions)

    alphabet or word cards (each child needs six)

    junk items (buttons, bottle caps, wiggle eyes, pipe cleaners, etc.)

    glue

    markers or pictures and scissors

Preparing for the Lesson:

Each pair of children decorates a milk carton with junk items to look like a robot. Allow robot to dry.

Each child selects six cards. Child draws or glues a picture of an object that has the same initial sound as that on the card. Teacher checks final work.

Grouping the Children:

Children are grouped by ability in pairs.

Activity:

Read *Now You Can Read About Robots* by H. Stanton (Brimax). After pairing the children, the two children get one robot, their own six cards and find a spot where they can work. The children exchange cards and take turns feeding the robot. The first child of the pair holds up a card and asks the other what it is. To find out if he/she is correct, the partner feeds the robot with the answer side up. Children may change partners for variety.

Center Activity:

Place your demonstration robot and one card from each child in a center where children can work together. Add new cards/concepts to the pile on a regular basis.

Remember:

Have the children say the words and look for the answer on the back of their own cards, checking themselves. Ask them which way was more fun and why.

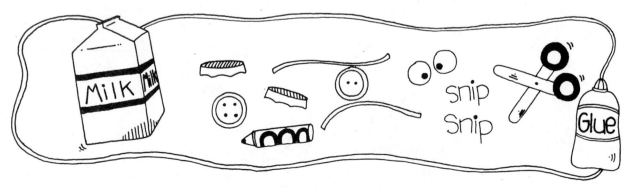

GA1395

Robot Directions

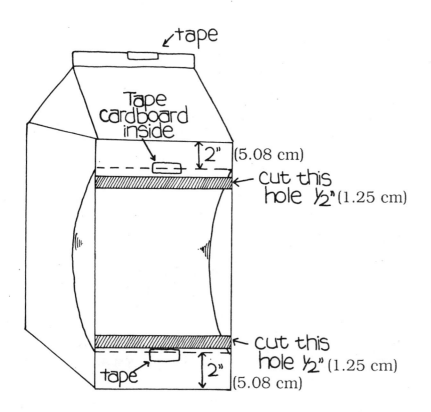

tape

Tape cardboard inside

2" (5.08 cm)

cut this hole ½" (1.25 cm)

cut this hole ½" (1.25 cm)

tape

2" (5.08 cm)

Mark — write name

Decorate

77

GA1395

Stegosaurus Soup

Soup made with dinosaur bones and vegetables is a treat for a cold day. Children each furnish a fresh vegetable for the Stegosaurus Soup. The teacher brings the bone, broth and cooked meat.

Materials Needed:

cooking pot	pan for washing vegetables
table knives	cutting boards
donated food items	serving bowls
spoons	serving spoon
hot pads	small containers
dish cloth and towel	

Preparing for the Lesson:

During circle time, children make a graph using the vegetables.

Discuss why vegetables are important for good health. Graph vegetables by type (roots, bulbs, stems, etc.) or by color or shape or weight. Compare weight of vegetables.

Grouping the Children:

Children work in groups of four or five.

Activity:

Discuss and demonstrate safety in cutting vegetables. Have children cut vegetables and put into small containers. Vegetables will be placed in large cooking pot when all have finished.

Cook the soup in a large crock pot. When the Stegosaurus Soup is finished, enjoy at snack time. Children should be responsible for helping with clean-up.

After clean-up, share a book with children such as *Stone Soup* by Marcia Brown. Discuss sharing with others.

If you are near a soup kitchen, taste the soup only and give it to the soup kitchen to feed the homeless.

Remember:

Talk with the children about their experience.

GA1395

Vegetables for Stegosaurus Soup

Look closely at all the food on this page.
Color only the vegetables.

If you have time:
Draw some fruits on the back of this paper.

GA1395

Pizza Factory

Children love to eat pizza, but seldom get the chance to see it made. You can have fun with your children as they work cooperatively making pizza in an assembly line. If you visit a pizza facility, use the activity as a follow-up to a visit to a pizza parlor.

Materials Needed:

refrigerator biscuits   6" (15.24 cm) foil squares   paint shirts
pizza sauce   onion   baking sheet
mozzarella cheese   green peppers   oven
black olives   pepperoni slices

Preparing for the Lesson:

Gather all the materials. If you have older children, they can chop the green pepper, slice the black olives, chop the onion and shred the mozzarella cheese.

Grouping the Children:

Divide the class into groups of eight. Set up the assembly line at two tables to accommodate up to thirty-two children, eight on each side of a table. Paint shirts are great cover-ups. Hats or hairnets are fun, too.

Activity:

Walk down the assembly line with the children demonstrating each job. Let them name the job as you demonstrate or use the names suggested. Label each job with a card.

Smasher   Flatten the refrigerator biscuit on a square of foil.
Painter   Brush pizza sauce on biscuit.
Sprinkler   Sprinkle mozzarella cheese on pizza sauce.
Dotter   Place three black olive slices on the cheese.
Pepperoni   Place two pepperoni slices on the cheese.
Green topper   Place green pepper pieces on the pizza.
White topper   Place the onion pieces on the pizza.
Inspector   Inspect. Shape foil into a circle. Place pizza on baking sheet.

Bake according to the directions on the biscuit container. Eat and enjoy. Make extras for others in the building.

Remember:

Have the children review the process with you and tell you how they worked together.

GA1395

To the teacher: Use these illustrations for badges or table signs when children are in their assembly lines. If you use it as a work sheet, cut off this top statement before copying.

Name_____

What Happened Next?

Color each of the pictures.
Cut out the pictures.
Put the pictures in order.
Write about each step below the picture.

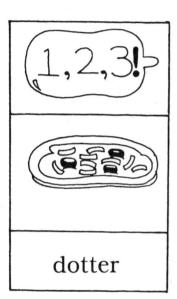

dotter

green topper

inspector

painter

pepperoni

sprinkler

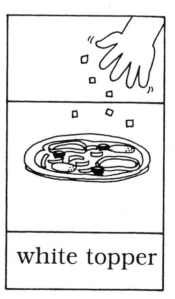

white topper

smasher

Note to the teacher: If your children come up with different job names, use them instead.

81

GA1395

Feed the Dinosaurs

Who knows what dinosaurs really looked like or just exactly what they ate? Even paleontologists will admit that they are making educated guesses. However, one thing we do know is that they were primarily meat eaters or plant eaters. While children do this activity, this concept is reinforced.

Materials Needed:

dinosaur pictures	vegetable pictures	3" x 5" (7.62 x 12.7
meat pictures	paper plates	cm) index cards

Preparing for the Lesson:

Copy the dinosaur pictures on the next page. Glue them to individual paper plates. Make sure that each group of children has one each of the dinosaurs.

Cut out meat and vegetable pictures from magazines, grocery ads or newspapers. Mount them on 3" x 5" (7.62 x 12.7 cm) cards. Make sure that each group has 20 to 25 pictures of food. (Have the children gather these in the days before the lesson.)

Grouping the Children:

Place the children in groups of four.

Activity:

Give each group of children four paper plates, each with a different dinosaur on it, an empty paper plate and a container of food cards. Starting with the youngest in each group and going to the left, each child will:

draw a card,

determine whether it is meat or vegetable,

check the response with the group,

determine whether the dinosaur the child has can eat it.

If it can, place it on the plate.

If it cannot, place it in the center of the group in the food kitchen (empty paper plate).

When all the food cards are gone, send the children to the food kitchen and have them figure out a fair way to distribute the rest of the food.

Remember:

Let the groups share how they solved their problem with the other groups when all are finished.

GA1395

Feed the Dinosaurs

Color each picture.

Cut it out.

Fold a piece of 9" x 12" (22.86 x 30.48 cm) construction paper into four boxes.

Glue one picture in the corner of each sheet of paper.

Tyrannosaurus Rex

Stegosaurus

Allosaurus

Triceratops

What Can I Eat?

Look at the pictures on the page.
Decide which ones you can eat.
Write the names of those you can eat by the picture of a child.
Decide which ones a stegosaurus could eat.
Write the names of those a stegosaurus could eat by the picture of the stegosaurus.

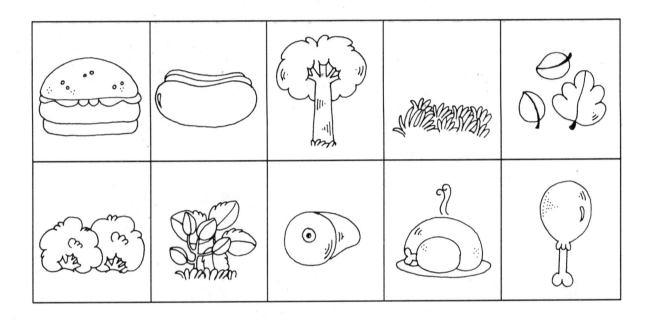

	A stegosaurus could eat:
	_____
	_____
	_____
	_____
	A child could eat:
	_____
	_____
	_____
	_____

GA1395

Clown Faces

Circus clowns create laughter for old and young. Children work together in pairs to make a clown face.

Materials Needed:

large sheet white paper with head shape

markers or crayons

cards with pictures of hats, hair, eyes, noses, mouths and ears

Preparing for the Lesson:

During circle time, have children share their experiences with clowns and the circus. Show pictures of sad and happy clowns. Discuss feelings.

Grouping the Children:

Group the children in pairs. Give each pair a sheet of paper, markers or crayons and a set of cards.

Directions:

Stack the cards on the table with the pictures face down.

Children take turns selecting a card. The first child selects a picture card from the top of the stack. The second child draws that part of the clown.

Change tasks and repeat until all the cards have been used.

Remember:

Share the products with the whole class. Each group of children can tell about how they made the picture. Each child can tell what part of the clown he/she made.

GA1395

How Does the Clown Feel?

Look at the clown.
Decide if you want the clown to be happy or sad.
Draw a face on the clown or paste on clown parts from next page.
Color the clown as directed.
Tell about your clown at the bottom of the page.

_____
_____
_____
_____
_____

GA1395

Clown Parts

87

GA1395

Measuring Mania

Children enjoy being actively involved in practicing measuring skills and comparing the lengths. As children explore their environment and compare/contrast common items with their friends, cognitive and social skills are gained.

Materials Needed:

1 piece of yarn for each group (different color and length for each group)

6 2" (5.08 cm) squares of construction paper for each group (color should match yarn)

masking tape

bag of objects to measure

Preparing for the Lesson:

During circle time, demonstrate the task of measuring. Pull items from a bag. Check for understanding by having children pass the items around the circle until they find the item that is the same length as their yarn pieces.

Grouping the Children:

Children will work in pairs.

Activity:

Each pair is given a piece of yarn. Each child is given three pieces of paper that are of the same color as their yarn. One child measures items in the room to find something that has the same length as the yarn. The other child checks the measurement and labels the item with a paper square.

Children continue taking turns until six items have been found. Extend this activity by finding items that are longer or shorter than the yarn.

Remember:

Discuss the activity in terms of working together. See if any parts were harder or easier. Which were the most fun?

GA1395

Recording Results of Measuring

Children can measure items with Unifix cubes and then transfer the measurements to a work sheet. They can then compare either the objects or the pictures of the objects to see which are longer, shorter or the same.

Materials Needed:

work sheet (on page 91)
bag of objects for each group
pencil   plastic spoon
bookmark   paint brush
plastic knife   crayons
Unifix cubes or 1" (2.54 cm) wooden or plastic cubes
task badges

Preparing for the Lesson:

Make bags of objects for the children and gather Unifix cubes for each group.

Present children with a stack of task cards and have them select a card for measuring, coloring or checking. They must get into groups where there is one of each task in the group.

Grouping the Children:

Children work in groups of three.

Activity:

Demonstrate
measuring objects using Unifix cubes.
placing the Unifix cubes on top of the work sheet.
removing one cube at a time and coloring the square.
checking coloring by putting the actual object that was measured on top of
     the colored squares.

Have children work in their groups on the tasks at hand, each checking the other.

Remember:

Review the process with the children for their input.

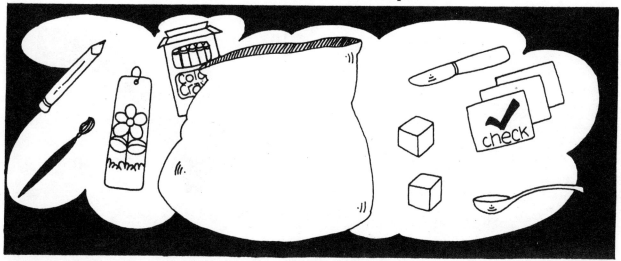

GA1395

Measuring Mania Task Cards

Measure

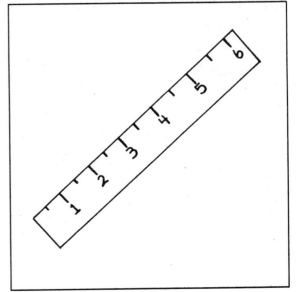

Color

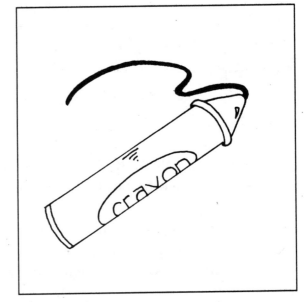

Check

GA1395

Just How Big Is It?

Names: _____

_____

_____

1

2

3

4

5

6

GA1395

Butterfly, Butterfly

Where Does the Butterfly Go When It Rains? by M. Garelick is a delightful way to introduce creative thinking and a fun art project. Children work together in pairs to develop thinking skills and to design butterflies.

Materials Needed:

a paper butterfly for each child
crayons or magic markers

Preparing for the Lesson:

During storytime read May Garelick's book, *Where Does the Butterfly Go When It Rains?* Pairs of children form buzz sessions to answer the question, "Where do butterflies go when it rains?" They then share ideas with the other groups.

Grouping of the Children:

Group the children in pairs.

Activity:

Give each child a folded paper butterfly pattern. Each child will design half of a butterfly. The designs are traded with the partner. The partner completes the butterfly by copying the original design. Display the butterflies on a bulletin board "Where Does the Butterfly Go When It Rains?"

Pattern and Book Options:

Try this at other times of the year with children designing a
Christmas tree - *The Christmas Tree That Grew* by Phyllis Kasilovsky
jack-o'-lantern - *The Biggest Pumpkin Ever* by Steven Kroll
Easter egg - *Golden Egg Book* by Margaret Wise Brown
All of these books are great for discussing cooperation.

Remember:

When children are finished with their patterns and have them displayed, have them discuss how they were made using cooperation.

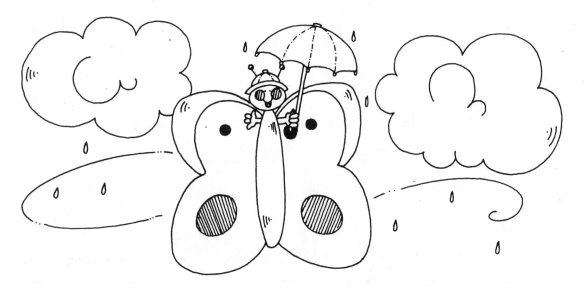

Just Like My Other Half

Read the color words.
Color half of the butterfly.
Make the other half just the same.

orange

red

yellow

brown

green

Butterfly
(Color this word any)
color you wish!

93

Copy Cats

What could be more fun than playing a game, but making the game first? Children work in pairs to construct a Concentration game of patterns using manipulatives that link together.

Materials Needed:

manipulatives that link together (links, Legos or Unifix cubes)

set #1 - 48 manipulatives in a variety of colors for builder #1

set #2 - 48 manipulatives (identical to original set) for builder #2

12 paper plates

Preparing for the Lesson:

Give each pair two sets of manipulatives and twelve paper plates.

Grouping the Children:

Group the children in pairs.

Activity:

1. Builder #1 makes a pattern using four manipulatives and places them on a paper plate.
2. Builder #2 builds an identical pattern and places it on another paper plate.
3. Children alternate this process using a new paper plate each time until six matching patterns have been constructed.
4. The teacher arranges the plates for Concentration by placing a pattern of manipulatives under each of the twelve paper plates.
5. Builders now play Concentration by taking turns lifting two plates to see if the patterns match. If a match is found, the child takes the manipulatives and the plates from the game. Continue playing until all the manipulatives have been removed.

Remember:

Talk with the children after the game about how they enjoyed it or worked out their problems.

GA1395

Is It Correct or Is It Incorrect?

Look carefully at each of the patterns below.
Some are correct. Some are incorrect.
Give a happy face to those that are correct.
Give a sad face to those that are incorrect.
Color the ones that are correct.

If you have time:
Put an X on the spot where the pattern is incorrect. On the back of the paper, draw patterns that make the incorrect ones correct.

95

GA1395

Rhyme Time

Children with different learning styles require activities that are varied in auditory, tactile and visual areas. Children working together in pairs use rhyming boxes to practice auditory skills using objects for tactile and visual learners.

Materials Needed:

rhyming box (shoe box) for each pair of children filled with objects and/or pictures that rhyme

Preparing for the Lesson:

Pairs of children sit on the floor and are given a box that contains rhyming objects.

Activity:

The first child closes his/her eyes and removes one object from the rhyming box and names it. The child returns to the box and looks for the rhyming object. If the children agree that the objects rhyme, the objects are placed on the floor. If the objects do not rhyme, the children continue the search together.

The second child repeats the process. When all the rhyming objects have been matched, the rhyming box may be exchanged for a new rhyming box.

Remember:

Review the process with the children.

GA1395

Feel for the Rhyme

Color and cut out the objects in the squres at the bottom of the paper.

Put the squares of paper in the rhyming box.

Color and cut out the objects in the squares at the top of the paper.

Put the squares of paper in the rhyming box.

Feel for the rhyme.

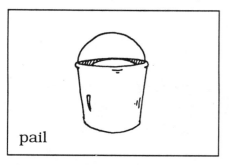
pail

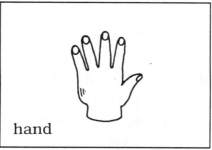
hand

jar

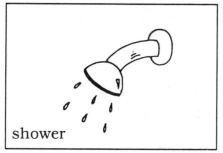
shower

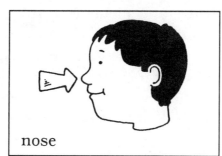
nose

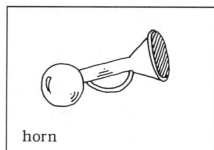
horn

bunny tail

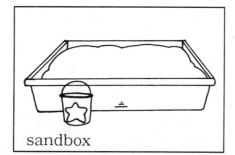
sandbox

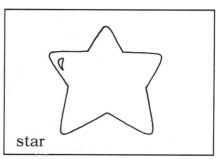
star

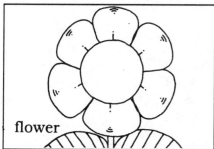
flower

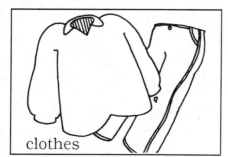
clothes

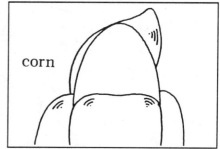
corn

Fish Pond

Students will work together in groups of three selected by the teacher. Their task is to practice grouping skills, use expressive language and practice fine motor coordination.

Materials Needed:

fishing pole with magnet on end of string

paper fish cards with pictures for classification (Vary this with the topic that you are studying, foods, animals, flowers, bugs, etc.)

paper clip on each fish card

designated area for pond

meat trays for sorting fish cards

Activity:

Read *One Fish, Two Fish, Red Fish, Blue Fish* by Dr. Seuss (Random House). Present the material to the children and demonstrate the process.

1. Discuss the fish cards, and then put them into the pond (picture not visible).
2. Introduce the meat trays, and model how these will be used to sort fish as a child pulls one from the pond.
3. Children in each group take turns catching a fish.
4. Children in each group work together to decide how to classify the fish. Children will find many different ways to classify fish.
5. The activity continues until all fish are caught and classified.

Remember:

At the end of the activity, ask children to tell why they put certain fish together. Ask if the fish can be grouped another way. Have children share grouping ideas in a whole group setting.

GA1395

Which Fish? Which Pond?

Look at all the fish around the edge of the paper.
Color them with bright colors.
See the two ponds?
Color them blue.
Cut out all of the fish.
Sort them into ponds.
Tell the teacher how you sorted them.
Label each pond of fish.

If you have time:
Ask the teacher for two sheets of blue paper to make into ponds. Make fish
from the scrap box. Ask a friend to separate the fish into two groups and put
them into the correct ponds.

GA1395

Watermelon Math

What fun to dig watermelon seeds out of watermelons. (But then, you can buy them at the seed store, too.) In this cooperative learning activity, children practice addition skills using watermelon seeds as manipulatives.

Materials Needed:

    10 large black watermelon seeds
    1 spinner (see page 101)
    1 work sheet (page 102)
    1 pencil
    1 felt watermelon slice (page 101)

Preparing for the Lesson:

Children will have experience with numbers 0 to 10 and understand how to tell a number story using addition. (More advanced children can use larger numbers on the spinner.)

Grouping the Children:

Organize the children in groups of four.

Activity:

Distribute materials and demonstrate tasks in the following manner.

The Spinner spins the spinner to determine the number of seeds to be placed on the watermelon slice.

The Counter counts the watermelon seeds and places them onto the watermelon slice.

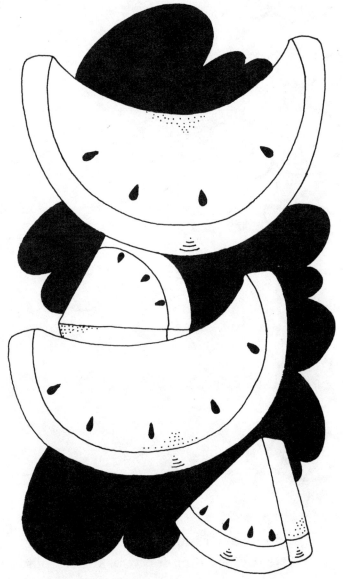

The Artist draws that number of seeds on the top of the work sheet.

The Writer writes the number of seeds on the bottom of the work sheet.

All children act as Checkers to count the total number of seeds and check the writer's sum.

Take turns telling a number story.

Remember:

When the children have completed their time allotment for this activity, review the process with them and have them tell you about working together.

GA1395

Felt Watermelon

Materials:

red and green felt, scissors and glue

Trace around the pattern onto green felt. Make a red center for the watermelon.

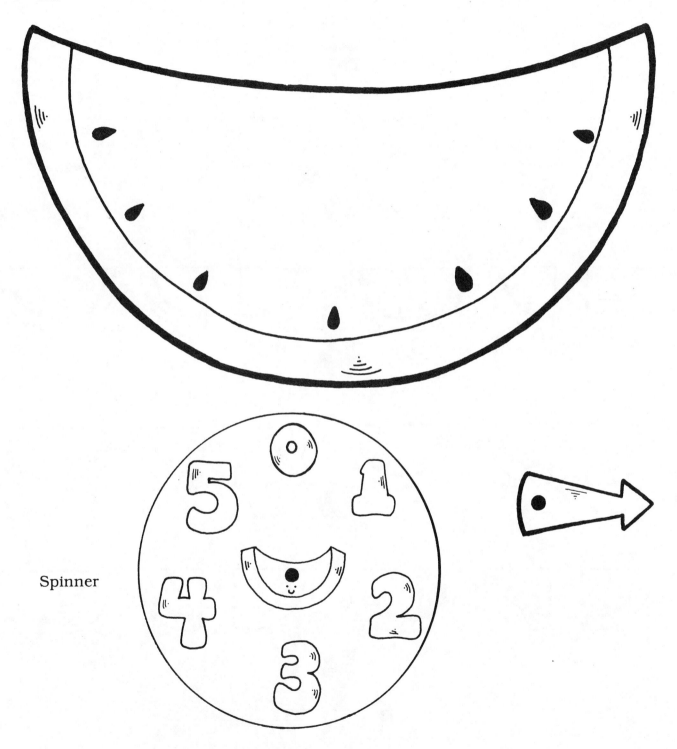

Spinner

Directions: Cut out the spinner. Mount it on heavy board. Laminate. Attach an arrow through the center with a brad.

GA1395

Watermelon Math
Work Sheet

Count the seeds.   Write the problem.

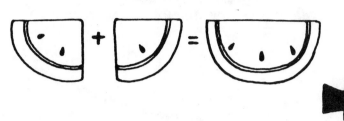 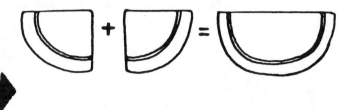

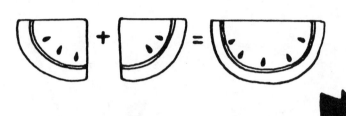 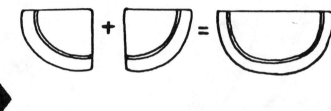

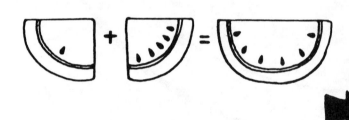 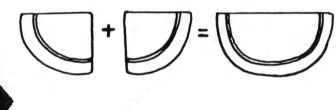

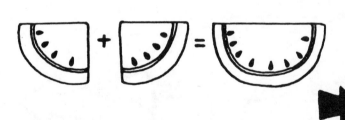 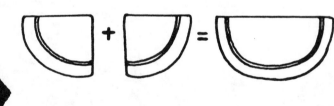

102   GA1395

What's New at the Zoo?

A zoo is a safe place where children can see wild animals in captivity. Children work together in groups of three using thinking skills to create imaginary animals for a classroom zoo.

Materials Needed:

cubes of Styrofoam packing   tape
6 golf tees   scissors
toilet tissue tube   sheet of newspaper
Styrofoam cup   sheet of tissue paper
6 pieces of yarn (24" [60.96 cm])   cotton ball
paper sack   small paper plate
3 sheets foil (12" x 12" [30.48 x 30.48 cm])

Preparing for the Lesson:

During circle time, read *Whingdingdilly* by Bill Peet. Discuss the body parts of the imaginary animals in the book. List the body parts found (head, body, legs, tail, ears, neck).

Grouping the Children:

Group the children in threes.

Activity:

Place a paper sack containing materials needed to create imaginary animals. Instruct children to open the sack of materials and begin thinking of ways to use the materials to create an imaginary animal. Construction begins after each child has shared at least one idea. Remind children that everyone works together and each one works to build a part of the animal.

Remember:

Review the fun with the children. Allow each child to tell you about the animal that was made.

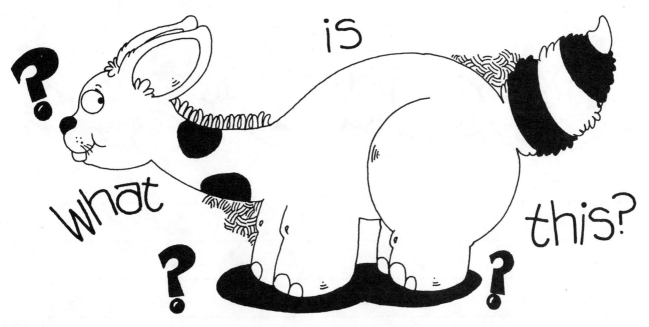

     GA1395

An Animal from My Imagination

Draw a picture of the animal you created.
Tell about the animal at the bottom of the page.

Draw your picture here ⬆

_____

_____

_____

_____

Dirt Cake

Dirt cake in flowerpots is uuummmh good, especially since the dirt is really chocolate cake crumbs and pudding! Children cooperate to assemble food for a special occasion or snack.

Materials Needed:

disposable 5 oz. (29.57 ml) clear plastic cups (flowerpot)
crumbled chocolate cake
chocolate pudding (mud)
gummy worms
lollipops (flowers)
plastic wrap
plastic spoons

Preparing for the Lesson:

After a demonstration of assembling Dirt Cake, six children work together assembly-line style.

Activity:

Job #1   Put 1/2" (1.25 cm) of dirt (chocolate cake crumbs) into the flower-pot (clear plastic cup).

Job #2   Put 1 tablespoon (15 ml) of mud (chocolate pudding) on top of the dirt.

Job #3   Put 1/2" (1.25 cm) of dirt on top of the mud.

Job #4   Place a candy worm on top of the dirt.

Job #5   Cover the top surface of the cup with plastic wrap.

Job #6   Poke flower (lollipop) into the top of the plastic wrap.

Remember:

Enjoy the snack with the children and listen to their comments.

GA1395

Job #1   Spoon 1/2" (1.25 cm) of chocolate cake crumbs into clear plastic cup.

Job #2   Spoon 1 tablespoon (15 ml) of pudding on top of crumbs.

Job #3   Spoon 1/2" (1.25 cm) of chocolate cake crumbs on top of the pudding.

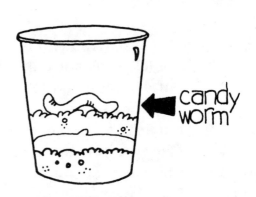

Job #4   Place a candy worm on top of the crumbs.

Job #5   Cover cup with plastic wrap.

Job #6   Poke lollipop into top of the plastic wrap.

GA1395

Picnic in the Park

P is for picnic. Pals work together in groups of four using coordination skills and cooperation to assist each other to the park for a picnic.

Materials Needed:

beanbag per child (color coded by groups)

obstacle course or trail for each group

picnic basket (one for each group if you can) filled with snacks that have initial sound of *P*: peanut candy, popcorn, pudding, pies, pocket pitas, peppermint, pickles

pink plastic plate for each child

Preparing the Lesson:

Give a beanbag of the same color to each person in the groups of four.

Activity:

Each group of friends will balance beanbags on their heads while traveling through an obstacle course or designated trail that leads to the picnic in the park. If a beanbag falls off someone's head, he/she is frozen until a friend from his/her group assists in returning the beanbag to his/her head. All the children in the class must reach the picnic area before the picnic of *P* snacks are prepared, identified and served.

Remember:

Write an experience story about the adventure. Put it up in the hall next to a giant *P* for all to see. Have the children cut out things that begin with *P* to place on the *P*.

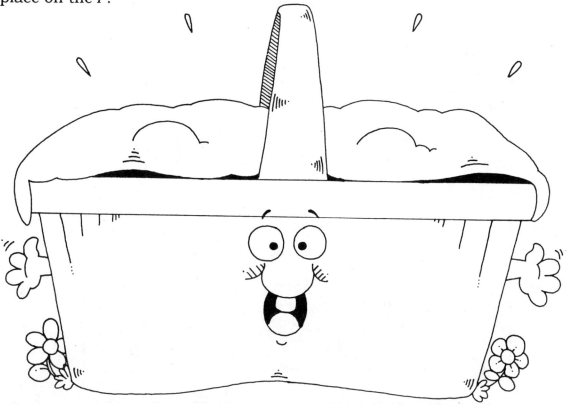

On a Pink Plate

Get a pink plate from your teacher.
Color all the pictures below that begin with *P.*
Cut them out.
Glue them to your pink plate.

Digging Up Dinosaurs

Students in groups of two will "dig for dinosaurs" and then construct an imaginary dinosaur using chicken bones.

Materials Needed:

Early in the year request parents' help in collecting clean chicken bones. Soak the bones in bleach for one day. Dry the bones for a couple of days. When ready for the lesson, bury bones in dishpans filled with rice; go outside and bury bones in clean sand or freeze them in large buckets of water. Tweezers, spoons, small brushes and hammers are tools that are necessary.

Preparing for the Lesson:

1. What is a skeleton? What does the skeleton do? Do other animals beside people have skeletons? Name some. Introduce rabbit or chicken bones (skeleton). What kind of bones are they? Why won't they stay together? Why do you need bones? Compare pictures or models of skeletons of humans, animals, dinosaurs.

2. Have children sort bones by shape. Try to identify bones relating to the human skeleton.

3. Play Simon Says to develop body awareness.

4. Using string and 34 pieces of macaroni, have the children make a model of the human backbone. It can be moved to show them the many positions the spine can take.

5. Sing the Skeleton Song . . . the ankle bone's connected to the leg bone, etc.

Activity:

1. Each group of two students digs carefully using a spoon and small brush as tools in the sand or rice or by using a hammer on the ice. Be very careful when digging into or chopping the ice. When children find an article (bone, etc.) place it on a tray with tweezers.

2. After "digging for dinosaurs," children continue to work together to invent an imaginary animal or dinosaur skeleton using the chicken bones and Play-Doh.

3. Children may cover the dinosaur with paper, fabric, etc.

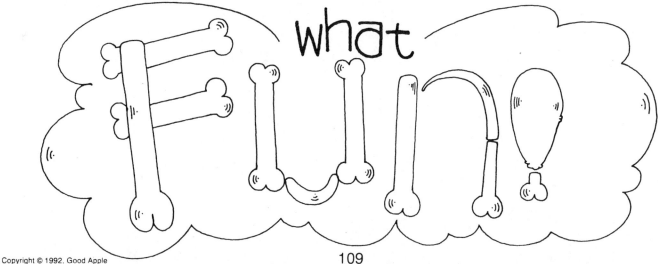

Name _____

What's Inside of Me?

This person looks empty.
Draw what you know is on the inside of a person.
Draw a face.

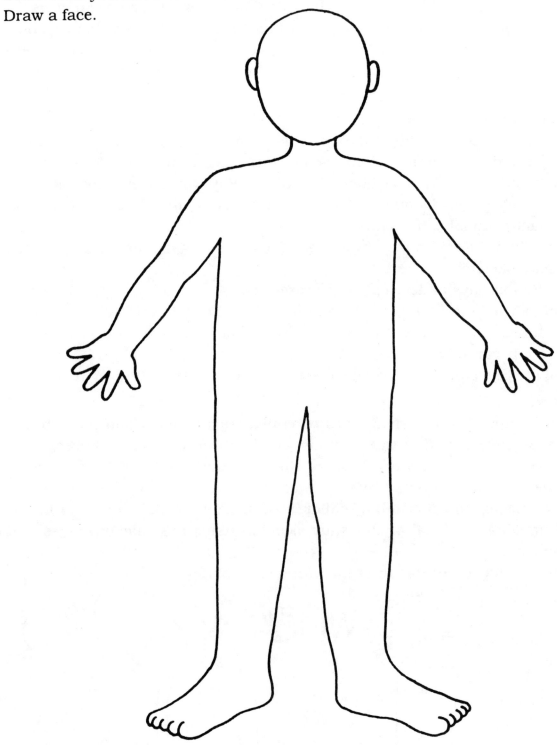

If you have time:
Use the scrap box and make clothes for this person.

110

City Engineers

Children become city engineers and develop their own city. This activity builds pre-map reading skills and can be extended to include traffic safety skills.

Materials Needed:

1/2 pint (.24 l) milk carton per child
construction paper scraps
scissors
markers
pencils
glue
large sheet of corrugated cardboard

Preparing for the Lesson:

The teacher draws city blocks and streets onto corrugated cardboard or a large piece of felt. Design the city so children will be able to reach all parts easily.

Discuss the project of planning and building a city. What buildings do we need in a town or city? Keep track of responses by labeling buildings on a large sheet of paper that can be cut apart.

Use a red marker to draw safety buildings, brown for shopping buildings, green for houses, blue for health buildings, orange for schools and libraries, purple for recreation, etc. Label the blocks with a specific color.

Grouping the Children:

Children will work in groups of four or five.

Whole Group Activity:

Assign a colored block to each group. Children discuss the buildings that would be in that category and each is assigned a task of constructing a building using a half-pint milk carton, construction paper and markers. The teacher will help label and glue the buildings onto the city block.

Add a school bus or other vehicle to the city and children will tell the class about their buildings and what you might see or do there as the vehicle passes by. This activity will familiarize the class with the city. Discuss the need for safety on the streets. Add safety signs where appropriate.

Center Activity:

Add vehicles and use as a play mat.

GA1395

What's in a City?

Look carefully at the blocks for this city. Color one block red for safety, one block brown for shopping, one block green for houses, one block blue for health, one block orange for schools, one block purple for recreation, one block pink for restaurants and one block yellow for entertainment.

Cut out the buildings at the bottom. Glue them onto the right spots.

112

Roly Poly Ice Cream

Making homemade ice cream is a tasty way to observe changing states of matter. Children use miniature homemade ice cream freezers and lots of cooperation to change a liquid into a solid.

Materials Needed:

One pair of mittens or gloves per child

Ice Cream Mixture
1 cup (240 ml) milk
1 cup (240 ml) cream
1/2 cup (120 ml) sugar
1 egg, beaten

Utensils
fork
1/2 cup (120 ml) measure
serving spoon
bowls
spoons

Materials for each homemade freezer
1-lb. (.45 kg) coffee can and lid
3-lb. (.45 kg) coffee can and lid
dippers for salt and ice
ice
coarse salt

Grouping the Children:

Children work in groups of four.

Activity:

1. Each child works assembly-line style adding one ingredient of the ice cream mixture to a 1-lb. coffee can (milk, cream, sugar, or beaten egg).
2. The teacher covers the 1-lb. coffee can with a plastic lid and helps children place the can of ice cream mixture inside the larger 3-lb. coffee can.
3. Children work together to pack layers of ice and salt around the can of ice cream mix.
4. The teacher covers the 3-lb. can with a lid.
5. Children put on gloves or mittens.
6. Children turn the can on its side and work together rolling the can back and forth to each other for approximately 15 to 20 minutes.
7. Direct observations of frost on the outside of the can, melting ice and the formation of ice crystals as the liquid mixture changes to a solid.

Remember:

Enjoy the snack and the wonder of the children.

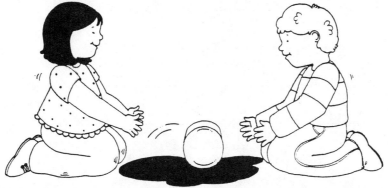

GA1395

Name _____

We Made Roly Poly Ice Cream

Look at the pictures and sentences.

Read the sentences.

They are in the wrong order.

Write the sentences in the correct order.

(Use the lines below, story paper or unlined paper.)

1. _____

2. _____

3. _____

4. _____

5. _____

6. _____

7. _____

GA1395

Don't Bug Me!

Ladybugs are fascinating to watch as they climb up a stem of grass or suddenly fly away. Children work together in groups of three to tell a subtraction number story about ladybugs that fly away.

Materials Needed:

10 ladybugs (large lima beans spray-painted red on one side and then decorated with black magic marker dots on both sides) (Ladybugs are red on one side and white on the other.)

flower garden (Have children make construction paper flowers and glue to green paper plates.)

3 ladybug headbands (Glue ladybugs to strips of yellow, black or green paper.)

shaker (a small cup you cannot see through)

Preparing for the Lesson:

Children make ladybug headbands.

Each child in the group has a different color headband. Children make a flower garden. Read *Life-Cycle Books: Ladybirds* (Longman).

Grouping the Children:

Divide children into groups of three. Each has a task.
Yellow is the Chooser. Black is the Shaker. Green is the Counter.

Activity:

Yellow: Chooses the number of beans to use.

Black: Puts the beans in a shaker, shakes them and tosses them into the garden.

Green: Picks up the red ladybugs, counts them and tells the group how many flew away.

The group then checks the garden to see how many are left. Older children can write the math problem they have created and solved.

Name _____

How Many Bugs?

Place bug stickers under each number in the equation.
Count how many bugs there are in all.
Write the answer in the box.

2   +   1 =

3   +   2 =

1   +   4 =

4   +   2 =

5   +   2 =

GA1395

Gone Fishin'

Jigsaw activities require careful management but produce involvement and cooperation of everyone. Children from groups of four go "fishing" for pictures of a specific category and return to sort their "catch."

Materials Needed:

4 badges of same color per group, each with a different category patch glued to the color badge (food, furniture, clothing, animals)

fishing pole with magnet per group

fish cards with category pictures (paper clip attached)

frying pan for "catch" (aluminum pie pan)

category sorting chart per group

Grouping the Children:

Divide children into groups of four. Give each child a badge. The badges of a group are all the same color. Each child in a group has a different category patch on his/her badge. This group is their family group.

Children rearrange themselves to form new groups according to the category on his/her badge. The new groups of four children are given a fishing pole.

Fish cards are placed in imaginary ponds on the floor in different areas of the classroom.

Activity:

1. Children who wear the same category patch work together to find fish cards with pictures of a specific category.
2. When no more fish of that category remain in that pond, children move to another pond.
3. Children divide the "catch" and return to the family group (same color badges).
4. The "catches" are placed into a frying pan. Children take turns removing fish cards from the frying pan and placing them on the sorting board.

Remember:

Monitor their placement in the various groups. Watch how they divide their "catches." Praise their efforts.

GA1395

Fish Come in Many Colors

Find a group of three other friends.
Have each friend choose a different color.
Color all of the fish on your paper with your color.
Cut out all of your fish.
Share them with your friends.
Everyone should have the same number of fish.
Glue them to a blue sheet of paper.

If you have time:
Decorate the fish with glue and glitter.

Magnet Magic

Children everywhere are fascinated with magnets. A simple discovery activity leads into classifying and sorting objects attracted and not attracted by a magnet.

Materials Needed:

magnet

box of objects - smaller magnets, paper clip, pinecone, clothespin, key ring (with metal and plastic or wood), keys, nails, washers, penny, pencil, toothpick, shell, thumbtack, toy car, spoon, ball bearing, bottle cap, rope, eraser, acorn, domino, rock, comb, Legos, buttons, etc.

puzzle task cards (see page 120; copy onto different colors of paper, one color for each group) (Put children's names on each section of the cards, one different child per task.)

erasable magic marker

sorting board (see page 121)

Preparing for the Lesson:

Read *Mickey's Magnet.*

During circle time, children identify and tell about magnets. The teacher demonstrates the task found on the puzzle task card (select an object, check object with magnet, and put object on sorting board). All of the puzzle task card pieces are placed in a pile on the floor or table.

Grouping the Children:

Children find a puzzle task card with their name and form groups of three with other children who have the same color puzzle task card. Children assemble the puzzle task cards and begin assigned tasks.

Activity:

Children select an object, check it with a magnet or put the object on the sorting board.

Remember:

Review the activity with them and talk with each group as they are working to see how well they are getting along together.

GA1395

Puzzle Task Card

Directions to the Teacher:

Duplicate, laminate and cut apart a set of puzzle task cards for each group of three children. Each group will need a different color of paper for their task cards. Assign tasks by writing a student's name on each laminated puzzle piece with water soluble marker.

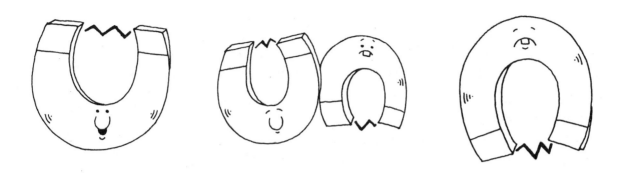

Yes   Both   No

Test your object with your magnet. Put it in the right place to indicate whether
or not the magnet attracts the object.

Follow the Footprints

Children's paper footprints can be an inexpensive and quickly made media for several math and reading activities. Working cooperatively, children make the footprints.

Materials Needed:

red or yellow 6" x 12" (15.24 x 30.48 cm) sheet of construction paper
orange or green 6" x 12" (15.24 x 30.48 cm) sheet of construction paper
pencil
2 pairs of scissors
12 cubes or links for measuring
magic marker

Grouping the Children:

Children work in pairs.

Activity:

Give each child a sheet of paper. Working in pairs, draw around your partner's shoe on a piece of construction paper using a pencil. Then let your partner draw around your shoe on another piece of paper.

Each child cuts out his partner's footprint. Help your partner write your name on your footprint. Measure your partner's footprint using cubes or other uniform material. Both count. Turn the footprint over and write the number of cubes long the footprint is.

Additional Activities:

1. Use partners. Compare the lengths of your footprints. Put a star on the one that is longer.
2. Put six children in a group. Order the six footprints from longest to shortest, etc.
3. Make a graph using long, medium and short as criteria for sorting. Help determine the length for each category.
4. Make a footpath using patterns of colors. When handing out the colored paper to make the footprints, consider patterning techniques.

GA1395

Name _____

Follow Those Footprints

Look at the maze below.

Help the children get home.

Color the footprints that will let them get home.

123

Follow That Footprint!

Several of these animals keep running into each other.
Color each animal a separate color.
Follow that animal's footprints to its home by coloring the footprints the same color.

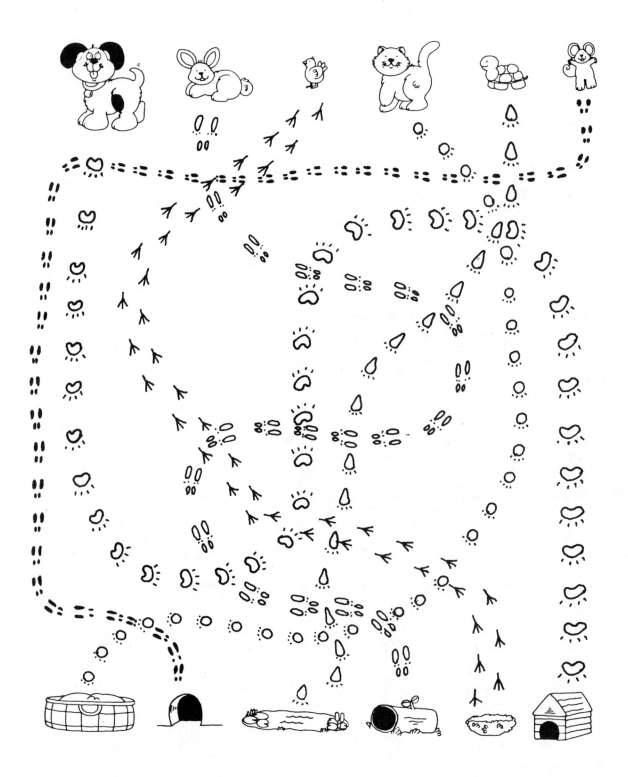

Gotcha Covered

Young children enjoy knowing how to read the names of their friends. Playing Gotcha Covered involves children in an independent activity that provides immediate feedback of answers. This activity may be constructed for use at different levels. Beginning readers may need names of children on their boards that start with different letters.

Materials Needed:

lotto puzzle board with 6, 8, 9, 10 or 12 spaces
answer cards
photocopies of children's photographs
wallpaper squares
answer sheet
envelope for answer sheet

Preparing for the Lesson:

Use a photocopy machine to make copies of photographs of individual children in a class. Lotto puzzle boards are constructed with a photo picture of a classmate in each space. Construct answer cards (name cards) with the names of classmates. Place the answer (name card) on top of the proper photo-picture. Turn the answer cards over so that no writing can be seen and glue a wallpaper square onto the back. The answer sheet is constructed by gluing an identical pattern of wallpaper squares to a sheet of paper and storing in an envelope. The envelope will accompany the lotto board.

Grouping the Children:

Each pair of children works together to cover a puzzle board.

Activity:

Children will take turns drawing a card with the name of a classmate and placing it on the matching photo-picture. The partner will check the answer or assist when needed. After children have covered all squares, take turns turning the answer cards over. Compare the block quilt-like design with the answer sheet. If the puzzle is correct, shake hands and say, "Gotcha covered." If the puzzle is not correct, remove pieces that do not fit and check answers. Children may use name desk tags as a reference if needed.

Remember:

Ask children how they helped each other find the names that matched the pictures. Compare likenesses and differences in names of children.

GA1395

Pattern Quilt

At the bottom of this page you see many squares.

Color the ones that match the same color.

Cut out the squares and lay them on the quilt to make a nice pattern.

When you find a pattern you like, glue the squares to the paper.

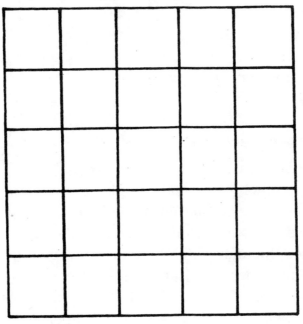

Color the matched patterns the same color.

Cut out the squares.

Make a design on the quilt above.

If you have more time:

Make a Place Mat

Design a place mat using crayons and graph paper (1" [2.54 cm] squares). Unifix cubes may be used to help design a pattern. Lift a cube and color with matching crayons. Option: Glue 2" (5.08 cm) squares of wallpaper, tissue paper, wrapping paper, shelf paper or newspaper to a sheet of paper to make a design. Laminate.

It's Just the Opposite

What's the opposite of sink? Float! What's the opposite of inside? Outside! Let the children respond orally and act our word opposites in a large group activity. When children are comfortable with the concept of opposites, introduce It's Just the Opposite lotto board game.

Materials Needed:

lotto board with pictures of word opposites
2 colors of game chips or markers
cards with pictures of word opposites

Grouping the Children:

Children will work in groups of three.

Preparing for the Lesson:

Construct the lotto boards by gluing pictures of word opposites onto each lotto board square. Make cards by gluing pictures that are opposite the ones on the lotto board onto cards that are cut the same size as the spaces on the lotto board. If preparing the game for advanced readers, use words on the cards instead of pictures.

Activity:

Children will work together to cover the lotto board with markers. One child draws a card and says the word opposite for the picture. The other two children take turns finding the opposite picture and covering it with a marker. Children may assist each other when needed. All children check each other's work.

Remember:

Monitor the children while working together. Children may work together at the end of the activity to draw posters of word opposites that can be used to make a big book. When the book is completed, children share their part of the book with the group. It is fun to check this book out to take home and share! If a large number of students are in a class, make more than one book.

GA1395

How Far Did the Inchworm Go?

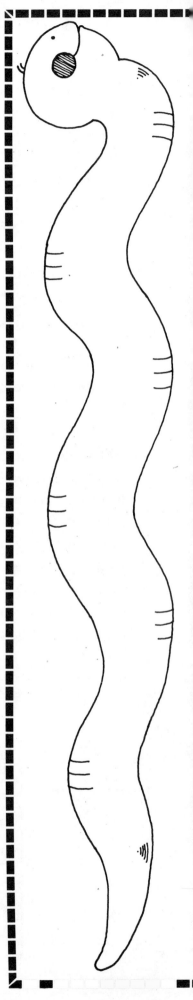

Leo Lionni's book, *Inch by Inch*, is used to introduce an activity of measuring, constructing a bar graph and comparing lengths. As the inchworm inches away from the many animals that would delight in eating him for a delectable treat, the children measure how far he goes. Remember to discuss the meaning of the story with the children before they do the measuring activity.

Materials Needed:

cards with pictures of animals that were in *Inch by Inch* (supplied by the teacher)
masking tape
bar graph (use graph from Old MacDonald)
green beanbag (represents inchworm)
measuring unit (paper inchworm)
several magic markers
masking tape "X" on floor or ground
task cards

Grouping the Children:

Children will work in groups of four, preferably outside or in a large room used for physical activity.

Activity:

Draw a task card. The Animal Keeper places an animal card on the X. The Thrower stands on the picture and throws a beanbag to show how far the inchworm inched away. The Measurer lays the inchworm measuring unit end to end and counts how far away the inchworm went. The Writer checks the counting and colors the corresponding number of boxes on the recording graph next to the picture of the animal. All children act as Checkers. (The Animal Keeper can use chalk to mark the place where the beanbag landed.) After the distance is recorded, children change tasks.

Remember:

Monitor the children as they work. Have the children share their graphs in a large group. Introduce vocabulary words: *farthest, closest, distance.*

GA1395

Old MacDonald Had a Farm

It's fun to sing "Old MacDonald Had a Farm" when the teacher dresses up like "Old MacDonald" and the children wear paper plate masks. Children find out which animal mask to make by making a graph using farm animals and then determining the animal which was chosen the fewest number of times.

Materials Needed:

bag

farm animal models or picture cards

materials for masks: paper plates, construction paper, glue, scissors, pencils, yarn, markers, paper punch

graphing grid with 4" (10.16 cm) boxes

Preparing for the Lesson:

The teacher makes a copy of the graphing grid below for each group.

Grouping the Children:

Children will work in groups of three.

Activity:

Children work together in threes taking turns pulling an animal from the bag and putting it on the graphing grid. After all the animals have been placed on the graph, the children determine which animal was chosen the fewest number of times.

Directions:

Children make paper plate masks of the animal that was least on their graph. Wear paper plate masks and sing "Old MacDonald Had a Farm" again. Have the children get into a circle. Children wearing a particular animal mask enter the barnyard (center of circle) when the song is about them.

Graph the Animals

At the bottom of this graph write names or draw pictures for animals you and your classmates made.

Count how many there were of each animal.

Color in that many squares above that animal.

Which animal had the most?_____

Which animal had the least?_____

Which animals tied?_____

Look at the pictures below. If you or your classmates made one of these animals, color it and cut it out. Glue it in the box below the graph.

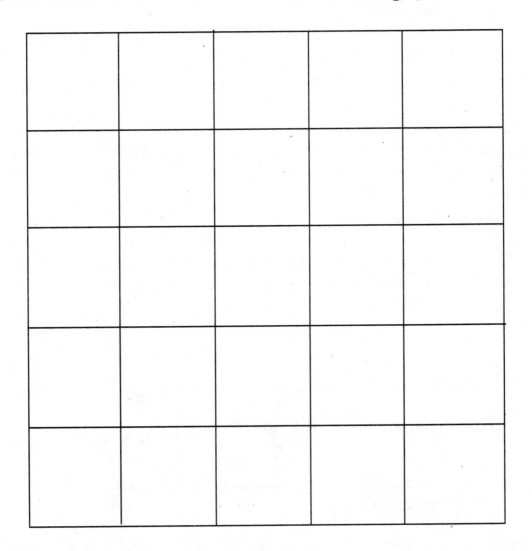

GA1395

Freckle Face

When the sun comes out, so do the freckles! Announce Freckle Day in advance by sending home a parent letter. Encourage children to wear clothing with spots to celebrate Freckle Day. Children decorate cookies with freckles. Use your imagination and let the children use theirs, too! Culminate the activity by reading *Freckle Juice* by Judy Blume over the next week.

Materials Needed:

    paper sun hung from ceiling
    mirror
    number cards (two per child)
    washable make-up pencils
    recording card

Preparing for the Lesson:

The teacher makes up number cards using numerals, dots or number words. While sitting under the sun, children take turns making freckles on their partners' faces. Each child has two number cards. The numbers on the cards tell the partner how many freckles to put on each of his/her friend's cheeks. Children may look at themselves in the mirror.

Grouping the Children:

Children work in pairs.

Activity:

Each pair of children makes a recording card that matches their partners' freckles. The number of freckles on one cheek are counted and then drawn in a circle. Repeat the process using the other cheek. Total the number of freckles and record by writing the number on the folded flap.

Remember:

Enjoy monitoring the activity. A camera could help the monitoring process. When the activity is completed, let the children share their freckled faces and their recording cards in a whole group.

Recording Card

GA1395

How Many Freckles?

Materials Needed:

    face page

    recording card (see page 131)

Directions:

    Cut out the face below. Glue it onto a paper plate. Get some red beans from your teacher. Get a partner. One of you will put freckles on one cheek. The other puts freckles on the other cheek. Count the freckles on your partner's cheek. Record it on a recording card. Have your partner count the freckles on your cheek. Record that number on the recording card. Count all the freckles together and record the answer.

If you have time, add hair, color face, etc.

GA1395

Where Is My Match?

Each of the objects below is in a square, circle, oval, triangle or rectangle.

When you find two objects that match, trace the shape around the object with one color. Do not use this color again. Continue until all the pairs have been traced in different colors.

Note to the teacher: Children will need a box of 16 different crayons in order to complete this page.

133

GA1395

It's in the Bag

Matching activities can be spiced up for many learning concepts and different levels of difficulty. It's in the Bag is a lotto game using both letter cards and manipulatives. Playing this game promotes interaction with others and an opportunity to reinforce letter sounds.

Materials Needed:

lotto board with 6-8 letters, pictures or words
cards with the same letters, pictures or words
bag with 10-15 objects

Preparing for the Lesson:

During circle time, model the activity using initial, medial or final sounds. For older children, use words and picture cards.

Grouping the Children:

Children will work in groups of three.

Activity:

Dump the bag of objects onto a mat. The Picker chooses an object and says the name of the object. The Hunter repeats the name of the object, finds the card, says the name of the letter and places it onto the matching letter on the lotto board. Each child is responsible for checking each other's work. After completing the lotto board, children signal the teacher for a final check. Trade the game materials with another group and rotate tasks.

Remember:

Monitor. Set up a quiet signal for children to use when needing your help or for checking work when finished.

GA1395

Play That Tune!

Music and children and reading go together naturally. Jars of water and a spoon can be used to create songs as children experiment with the various pitches and amounts of water in the jars. Children can then use their reading skills to recreate the songs. This music is original and fun.

Materials Needed:

4 baby food jars
metal spoon
small pitcher or milk carton of water
food coloring
Unifix cubes or 1" (2.54 cm) connecting cubes
markers
3' (.91 m) strip of adding machine paper
masking tape

Grouping the Children:

Children work in pairs.

Preparing for the Lesson:

Give each pair of children four baby food jars. Each jar has a few drops of food coloring in the bottom. Children take turns pouring the amount of water they want into the jars. Children arrange the jars in order from most water to least water.

Activity:

Children work in pairs to create songs by tapping the jars with a metal spoon. After they practice, they take turns creating and recording a song.

As one child plays a song, the other selects a Unifix cube that matches the color of water and places it on long strip of paper which has been taped to the tabletop. Then the children work together to color the song pattern onto the strip of paper by lifting a Unifix cube and coloring a spot with that color of marker.

Children take turns playing the song by looking at the song pattern. After they have played their own tunes, they can play someone else's tune.

GA1395

Spell These Words

Look at the word on the left side of the paper.
Copy it on the right side of your paper.
If there is not a word on the left side, look at the bottom of the paper.
Copy a word from the bottom onto the left side of the paper.
Copy it again on the right side of the paper.

1. _____   1. _____

2. _____   2. _____

3. _____   3. _____

4. _____   4. _____

5. _____   5. _____

6. _____   6. _____

7. _____   7. _____

8. _____   8. _____

9. _____   9. _____

10. _____   10. _____

Directions for the teacher: Print spelling words for the children on the odd lines
at the left and different ones in the five boxes below.

Spelly Nelly

Practicing spelling words is boring for many children. Card games like "Old Maid" can easily be adapted to provide spelling practice. Children are so busy working, they don't realize they are learning their spelling words.

Materials Needed:

4" x 6" (10.16 x 15.24 cm) index cards
list of spelling words
1 marker
1 card with picture of "Spelly Nelly"

Preparing for the Lesson:

Introduce the spelling lesson. Prepare a card with a picture of "Spelly Nelly" for groups of four children.

Grouping the Children:

Children work in pairs to make two sets of spelling words. Children then join another group and play the game in groups of four.

Activity:

Working in pairs, children take turns copying a spelling word onto a card using a marker. Children then check each other's work. When all of the spelling words from the list have been copied, each pair joins with another pair to form a new group. Combine all the cards to make a card game to be played following the same rules as "Old Maid" using "Spelly Nelly" instead.

Color Spelly Nelly.
Glue Spelly Nelly to a 4" x 6" (10.16 x 15.24 cm) index card.

Spelly Nelly

GA1395

Follow That Path

Follow the path with your pencil that each animal follows.
At the bottom of the page, list the things each animal passes.

raccoon   mouse   dog   squirrel

_____   _____   _____   _____

_____   _____   _____   _____

_____   _____   _____   _____

_____   _____   _____   _____

_____   _____   _____   _____

GA1395

Cartographers (Map Makers)

While learning the importance of maps, children participate in a hands-on activity of making a map of their classroom. A real cartographer must develop skills of visual discrimination, position, number concepts and directionality. Special pictures of items found in the room provide an opportunity for a child's early concept of map making.

Materials Needed:

pictures of chairs, tables, doors
    clocks, calendars, windows,
    bulletin boards, chalkboards
large sheet of paper
glue
scissors

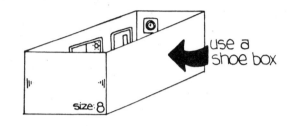

use a shoe box

Grouping the Children:

Children will work together in groups of three.

Preparing for the Lesson:

Gather children in a large group and show a shoe box model of a bedroom. Demonstrate how to make a map of the bedroom.

Discuss why people need maps. Tell about people who make maps (cartographers).

Activity:

Each child will count a specific item in the room, cut that item out of a work sheet, and paste onto the room map. One child is responsible for chairs, another for tables and another for the remaining items.

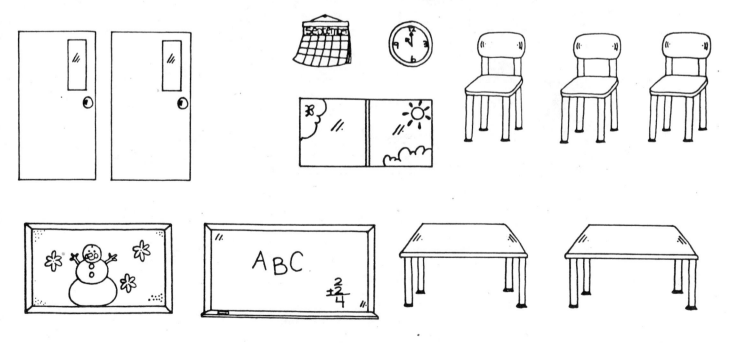

GA1395

Opposites Again

Color and cut out each of the pictures.

Pair up the opposites.

Glue one picture in each pair to a piece of cardboard in random order.

Glue the other picture of each pair to a piece of construction paper.

Find the matches on the board and cover them with the opposite picture card.

140

GA1395